God Never Fails

BY

Mary L. Kupferle

DEVORSS & COMPANY
P.O. BOX 550, MARINA DEL REY, CA 90294-0550

CONTENTS

The Grace of God Is upon You

WHATEVER your appointed tasks may be this day, go forth rejoicing, knowing that the grace of God is upon you! Before you set your hand to any task, before you take any action, use a few moments to remind yourself of this truth and affirm quietly, in faith, *"I go forward joyously, for the grace of God is upon me."* You will find your accomplishment of your tasks easier than you had thought possible, your efforts abundantly fruitful and rewarding.

In telling us of the boy Jesus, Luke says, "The child grew, and waxed strong, filled with wisdom: and the grace of God was upon him." This same grace, dear friend, is not reserved for Jesus only, but is given freely to every growing, unfolding child of God throughout eternity. The watchful Father is as eager to pour out His love upon you and me as upon Jesus Christ, for He knows and sees us, each one, as a son of His own creation, image of His own Being, worthy of His tenderest benediction.

Because we are all sons of God, we are free

to recognize and accept the grace, the love, of God in the same full measure just as Jesus did. Because you are a son of God, you are meant to assume the same attitude, manner, and bearing that you feel Jesus Christ Himself assumed in His earthly ministry. You are meant to act in the same manner as He, and you can, because the grace of God is upon you! You are meant to conduct yourself with the same dignity, having the same spiritual assurance you know He had, and you can, because the grace of God is upon you!

If something extremely difficult seems to be required of you, if you are faced with a trying situation, condition, or circumstance, set aside all doubts and fears right now, and for a few moments simply acknowledge your own divine sonship. Declare in faith: *"God loves me. His grace is upon me, and only good can come."*

Let the words *"His grace is upon me"* move through your thoughts; speak them aloud, then relax and accept them throughout your whole being. God's grace is upon you, upon your mind and its activity, upon your body and its functions, upon your life and affairs. God's grace is upon you now, blessing you, encouraging you, helping you, uplifting you, sustaining you, protecting you, guiding and directing you.

Wherever your duties take you, the grace of God is upon you. Wherever your duties keep you, the grace of God is upon you. However distasteful, unappealing, routine, monotonous, unrewarding your work or assignment may seem, the grace of God is upon you, and His blessings pour through you. However demanding, however filled with responsibility your appointment, the grace of God is upon you, and you are filled with new wisdom and confidence.

Because the grace of God is upon you, the dignity of Christ, the serenity of Christ, hold you poised; the love of Christ keeps you gracious and compassionate; the competence of Christ leads you into success and satisfaction.

The grace of God is upon your hands as they serve, regardless of the capacity in which they serve. If your service seems menial and humble, the grace of God will transform that service into a ministry to the glory of God. If your service seems of great importance to the world, the grace of God will lend to that service a humility and beauty that glorifies not personality but Spirit.

Know that the grace of God is upon every thought you think, every word you speak, every step you take; is upon your every action, decision, and movement. As you realize this, your thoughts will be clear, illumined; your words will be convincing, faith-filled; your actions will be spiritually significant, blessed.

Recognize, accept the wonderful truth that God loves you, that His grace is upon you as you grow and wax strong in spiritual expression. The grace of God is upon you this day, this hour, this moment. It is upon your body temple, upon your business, upon your home, upon your entire life, and you are blessed, blessed, blessed! The grace of God is upon you now!

God Never Fails

THE FOUNDER of the famous Bristol, England, orphanages, George Müller, lived by his faith that, whatever the need, God never fails. Over a period of some sixty years, he was able, through this faith, to build and maintain homes for more than two thousand orphans, able to raise nearly one and a half million pounds without asking anyone for a penny, able to be daily a living example of the goodness of God.

At one time he remarked, "Not once, or five times, or five hundred times, but thousands of times in these threescore years, have we had in hand not enough *for one more meal,* either in food or in funds; but not once has God failed us; not once have we or the orphans gone hungry or lacked any good thing."

It is said that this faith-filled man never made auxiliary arrangements in case supplies did not arrive; he dug no second-line trenches. He had no outer friends to turn to, none on whom he could depend for assistance. All he did possess was a vital, living, active faith that he put to use day by day, hour by hour, minute by minute in everything he desired to accomplish. He simply believed that God was his one and only source of supply, unfailing and inexhaustible, and he tested and proved the truth of his belief.

Whatever it is that you today are attempting to prove in your life, whether it concerns health, supply, or harmony, remember, God never fails! You need not depend on human judgments, upon personal opinions, upon outer circumstances and outworkings, but simply, only, upon God, the one Source, the one Giver, the one Creator of all good. Cease to depend any longer upon appearances, upon human reasoning and logic, and depend wholly, absolutely, on God.

Repeat to yourself over and over, both silently and aloud, *"God never fails."* Take this thought into your heart this very moment, and repeat it again and again: *"God never fails. God never fails. God never fails."*

Keep repeating the words quietly but firmly and confidently: *"God never fails. God never fails."* Say them with all the faith you can muster. Repeat them with all the determination and conviction you can call upon from the very depths of your being. Hold to the truth they express, in spite of any outer conflict. Maintain your stand, regardless of any lashing of the winds and waves of the senses. Let this truth be the rock upon which you stand. Let it form the beginning, the foundation of a new and strong and indomitable faith, a faith that is your own divine birthright.

You need not try to figure out how the situation can change and right itself. It is not up to you to look ahead to tomorrow or next week and to know in advance all the various details. You are not to be anxious and consider how, when, why, who—your only part in the working out of your problem is to be still, take your stand, and know that God never fails.

Steadfast in this state of mind, you are not anxious, no matter how many persons, things, or conditions on the outside seem to fail you, for in themselves these do not matter. All that does matter is God! And God is the same unchangeable, unvariable, loving Father now that He always has been. He is the same perfect Presence and Power today as when Jesus called upon Him two thousand years ago. He is the same dependable Creator and Sustainer, infinitely willing to bless, to heal, and to prosper every one of His children, now and forever.

A Truth student who had been depending upon a certain source for a sum of money to handle an obligation was severely disappointed and discouraged when the source failed to produce as expected. In the very moment of discouragement, however, the student summoned all the faith at his command, declaring aloud: *"God never fails. Human channels may seem to fail, vary, or change, but God never does. God never changes. God never fails."*

Throughout the remainder of the day, this student maintained this attitude and clung to the truth, *"God never fails."* Again and again he repeated the words, affirmed them, believed them. Within less than twenty-four hours, the needed amount was forthcoming from an unexpected, entirely different source. No matter what faces you, God never fails. He will not fail you in your dilemma. He will not fail you in your challenge. The only demand He makes upon you is that you have implicit trust in Him. You are to turn wholly and completely to Him and Him only. You are not to give one smattering of attention elsewhere. Not one jot or tittle of your devotion is to be turned to outer things. All your heart, all your mind must be centered in just one place—God!

If you will follow through with this extremely simple method of prayer and hold to it unwaveringly, you will prove for yourself that God does not fail. You will find that your faith is strengthened in the process, that your good becomes manifest in greater benefits than you even dreamed.

A consciousness of light, an awareness of spiritual illumination, is the first step in the healing of any personal difficulty, even as it was the first step in the process of creation. "And God said, Let there be light: and there was light." It was after this, after the coming of the light, that the other steps of creation followed, all in the divine order that is typical of God and His nature of perfection. The true spiritual light, our first step in understanding and overcoming, is worth awaiting in our silent periods of prayer, worth our time and patience and application of faith, even as the dawn is worthy of all nature's quiet attention. The awakening of our souls anew to eternal spiritual truths and values cannot come any other way.

Sometimes this awakening comes immediately, forcibly, within a prayer. Sometimes it comes gently, almost unnoticed, after we have prayed and then attended to the things at hand. Someone told recently of the way in which the light entered her consciousness during the healing of a loved one. She said that for a number of days she declared both silently and audibly the spiritual truths she knew regarding the dear one's divine inheritance of wholeness and perfection. She believed the person could be healed and was faithful in the application of all Truth principles she knew. But it was finally upon her firm declaration, "Let there be light!" that full realization came and the physical healing became apparent.

The Truth student mentioned that at this point of declaration something within her consciousness was awakened, that even as she stood at the ironing board the light so flooded her consciousness as to make all things new and clear. She explained that it was a realization that all that had gone before was passed and was nothing. She had a firm conviction of healing that no human reasoning or intellectual argument could affect.

She was no longer concerned with appearances or anxious about results, but simply convinced of the good and the true within the situation. The light had entered her consciousness through complete devotion to God the good. Her thoughts were awakened to the Truth of Being through singleness of inner vision. The outer demonstration followed.

There is no difficulty so dark that it cannot be clarified by the light of the indwelling Christ, the light of Truth. There is no problem of the physical being so deep that this light cannot reach it, touch it, and transform it. There is nothing in all our lives too confused for the light of Truth to make plain. We can, at the moment we are willing to become single-eyed, declare, *"Let there be light!"* and there will be light. We will see the light concerning every situation of mind, body, and affairs. And we will find the relief, the upliftment, the healing, and blessing our hearts desire.

When Jesus healed the beggar who had been blind since birth, the beggar was plied with questions by the Pharisees who could not believe him or that he truly had been healed so quickly, so simply and unpretentiously by the

Master. His answer to all their queries was: "I know not: one thing I know, that, whereas I was blind, now I see." He saw light while he had been in darkness, and there was no human reasoning that could account for it. The answer is in the singleness of spiritual vision within Jesus. Where there is one with such purity of heart, devotedness of soul, one-pointedness of consciousness, the light is radiant to bless, heal, and uplift all who come within its presence and will receive.

Such was the divinity within Jesus, the Christ light within Him. And such it can be within you and me today if we will apply our attention, devote our efforts, and become as little children—teachable, obedient to inner guidance, watchful of our words and actions, ready to discipline and to master according to the Christ example. Day by day we prove this through the time we give to prayer and meditation. Day by day we prove this by our thoughts and words and actions.

The more we pray, the oftener we turn our thoughts to God, and the more light becomes evident. The more we meditate about the meaning of Jesus' teachings, the more enlightened our consciousness becomes. The higher we raise this light in our words and actions, the more Christlike our words and actions become. The more steadfastly we look to the Father as the source of our wisdom and illumination the more open we become to receive His luminous blessings, the more aware we become of our spiritual identity, the more clearly we behold spiritual reality—the Christ within everyone, God in everything.

This light abides within you now, dear friend, as the illumination you desire for the overcoming of every difficult situation in your life. It is God's gift to you, awaiting your returning to Him in consciousness, your awareness of His nearness and love. Lift up your heart to Him in prayer now, in this moment, and decree, *"Let there be light!"* and your eyes will be opened to the reality of good, the reality of wholeness, wisdom, happiness, and abundant well-being. The light will enter your consciousness, and you will see the Truth within your heart, for that is the place of the overcoming. There lies the victory; there abides the "light of the world."

Meditation for Self-Help

Let us face that problem confronting you right now! Let us look at it squarely and see it in its true light and take it for its true worth. No matter how long it has hampered your perfect expression of health or peace or success, let us now refuse to believe in failure or discouragement. Its appearance in your life is actually a shadow, temporarily darkening your thoughts and your day. It is only in your thoughts that you are bound and deceived by error and unhappiness.

There is one sure way to cut those ties, child of God; and it is so simple and easy and perfect a way that we are apt to pass it by and look for a more arduous and difficult one. But it is in the simplicity of divine law that all things are made plain.

Become as a little child, meek, and humble, willing to be guided by your Father and Maker. Free yourself from the tight, cramping style of vain struggle and let, just let, His will be done in you! Relax and turn your face to the sunlight, as the shadows fall behind. As you still all noise and clamor and focus your attention on the magnificence and glory of the Father's word, on the blessed assurance of His ever-loving care and guiding hand, part of this heavenly blessing will seep into your heart and mind and body.

When through your complete acceptance of divine law the clear, full light of Truth and wisdom are permitted to shine forth, all shadows will dissolve. Then the shackles that bound you will lose their power and suddenly drop and fade into nothingness.

Stand straight and strong and free, unfettered and unbound, acknowledge your divine and glorious heritage of health and plenty, peace and joy, the birthright that was yours from the beginning and now awaits your acceptance. Hear your Father's promises:

"Thou shalt also decree a thing, and it shall be established unto thee."

"All things whatsoever ye pray and ask for, believe that ye receive them, and ye shall have them."

"Ask, and ye shall receive, that your joy may be made full."

Begin with God

RECENTLY I had the opportunity to see a magnificent diamond called the "Shah of Persia," said to be worth half a million dollars. About four inches in circumference and one inch in depth, it throbbed in its setting with liquid fire as though alive. The constantly changing, sparkling colors were unforgettably beautiful.

Later that same day, looking over the rows of newly trimmed grapevines in the garden, I noticed the sap had begun to rise, and every pruned branch was starting to exude large globules of moisture. As the vine stirred, these globules caught the sunlight and flashed with a blinding brilliance surpassing even that of the famed "Shah of Persia." Diamonds out of the earth, into jewel, into vineyard, each beginning with the same source, God, the originator of all beauty! "Looking upon the grain of sand, we cannot tell how it cometh or whither it goeth, but we know that it is forever held in the bosom of the whole, the same as are the stars in the heavens and the gold in the earth."

So it is that all goodness, all beauty, all truth starts with God, flows forth forever from the heart of God, whether it be in the form of a lovely jewel, a shining cluster of grapes, a towering pine, the phosphorescent beauty of the midnight ocean, a flaming sky, the melody of lark or mocking bird; whether it be abundance, joy, or radiant well-being for you and me, the highest-endowed of all God's creations.

Thus it is, beloved, that to become aware of perfect health and strength we must begin where all health and strength begin, with God, the infinite source of eternal well-being. Thus it is, beloved, that to be conscious of radiant happiness and contentment we must begin with God, the author of divine fulfillment. Thus it is, beloved, that to know unfailing supply we must begin with God, the originator of everlasting abundance.

It is only by beginning with God that we can behold the solution to all difficulties, only by starting with God that we can behold the truths about His kingdom and His children. It makes no difference what anyone appears to be or do, what it seems impossible for anyone to be or do, what changes are required in order to solve a problem, what transformation must be made in order to bring about light and understanding, peace and happiness. If we start with God it will be done!

Early one evening several years ago an incident occurred that reminded me of this truth. After returning home from a meeting with a group of young people I saw that one of the colored stones in a small pin was missing. Although an inexpensive piece of costume jewelry, the pin was a favorite one, and I had hesitated earlier that day to leave it on the coat lapel. On second thought however I had denied the suggestion of loss and gone on my way, walking five blocks to the bus stop, riding to school, meeting with the children in the schoolroom, then conducting outdoor activities on the cinder playground.

Reason and logic protested against the possibility of finding the small blue stone, but again I rejected the thought of loss and knew that if I "began with God" the stone would be found. Silently, humbly I asked the Father to show me how to proceed. Promptly following His inner guidance I returned to the school, walked across the grounds toward the school steps, and at the first downward glance saw the stone directly before me.

Every day we have many small opportunities like this, and others that are greater, where we can begin with God and behold His love becoming manifest in our life or in the lives of those about us. Let us awaken to the fact that we need not listen to personal reason and human logic but only begin with God to prove the reality of good. Let us awaken to the truth that we need not "know more about the situation" in order to proclaim victory over it, that we need not "understand all the angles" in order to know divine law, that we need not work with physical reason and cause but only with God, who is the only cause and action and effect within the universe.

On another occasion, when mention was made of a loved one suffering from emotional upset, it again became very clear to me that, even though I knew little about helping others to demonstrate health, I must use the small understanding I had by beginning with God, the eternal source of all stability. "And where," I thought, "is this stability but in the very place where confusion seems to exist!"

Centering my thought on the loved one I affirmed for her that all was divine activity and peace, and that right where I was I could most easily "begin with God." As I learned later on, within a few moments after that the young woman had noticed an inner warmth and activity stirring and loosening all tension and disturbance, permitting her to partake of nourishment and to continue immediately with her physical work.

When the appearance of illness or pain presents itself, we can begin either with limited reason and logic and cause, or by turning our heart to God, the author of unlimited and perfect health. When someone is unkind or critical, we can begin either with resentment and self-pity, or by turning our heart to God, the author of love. When the appearance of lack tends to arouse inharmony, we can begin either with faultfinding and condemnation, or by turning our heart to God, the author of abundance. When emotions upset and frighten us we can begin either by running from the situation, or by turning our heart to God, the author of peace and power.

What is your problem right now, beloved?

How does the number of times you have thought of it, its appearance of cause and effect, compare with the number of times you have thought of God today? As soon as the weight of our thought about God overbalances our thought about negation, our good will become manifest. Greater understanding of a problem, no matter what the problem may be, will not serve to help us to understand God more readily, to work with God. Only by thinking of Him, by returning to Him again and again in consciousness, shall we be able to work with Him.

Still our impatient hearts may cry: "But this habit of thinking of God is so slow in developing. I want to know the source of my good now!" This is a natural protest, and it arises within each of us who wants to claim his heritage as God's son and heir. But the whole step cannot be taken in one immediate realization, for we have willfully traveled afar in consciousness from the Father's house, and divine awareness must be regained in diligence and patience.

Suppose we wanted to renew a friendship with someone we knew years ago. Would we expect to know once more in one short moment at first meeting the entire nature of that person?

Would we expect to regain that relationship without further visits with him, without devoting time and thought to him, to his ideas and interests? Of course not! Neither can we expect to regain awareness of the divine relationship between ourselves and our heavenly Father except by living with Him in consciousness, by thinking of Him, of His nature, and of His Fatherhood to us.

I know a very fine and brave person who, over a period of many years, has traveled constantly to visit dozens of persons and places in search of a healing of a seeming ailment. Each time a different solution is presented, and each time the solution fails, leading her to fix her attention on other symptoms and to start another search for a different kind of healing. She is not yet ready to begin with God, to accept the truth that God is the answer of perfect health and wholeness, the one answer to every question and doubt and difficulty. Her attitude toward the heavenly Father is like that of the little girl who protested indignantly, "I don't see what 'nature' has to do with the out-of-doors."

Again and again our blind personal will leads us away from the truth that we "began with

God," that we are now and forever centered in God. While the truth of this divine relationship is beheld only dimly, the eternal bond between Father and son is felt only occasionally. Beloved, do you too sometimes wonder what God "has to do with" your health and wholeness, supply and happiness? Believe this: He is your health and strength and sufficiency of every good thing! As God's children and heirs we are all basically and spiritually as inseparable from God our Father as nature is from the out-of-doors. Everything we think and feel and do should arise from a consciousness of our being forever centered in Him.

Let us awaken to the Master's way of living, the way of radiantly joyous, successful living, by realizing that the only starting point in dealing with any circumstance, condition, or situation is God! No matter what we desire to demonstrate, if we will begin with God, good will result. Regardless of the appearance of any kind of ill-health, the only starting point of all life is God, and all that emanates from God can be only good. Regardless of the appearance of any kind of lack, the starting point of all activity is God, and all that emanates from Him can be only abundance. Regardless of the appearance of any kind of frustration or emotional disturbance, the only starting point of all expression is God, and all that emanates from Him can produce and result in only joy and well-being and stability.

Whatever your problem, beloved, begin with God, in your own way and your own words and your own prayers, the way that is simplest and easiest for you, and your heart's cry will be answered! Only begin with God! Even if you have tried many many times before this moment, try again to begin only with God, and you will behold Him in the midst of your problem!

Every seeming difficulty or failure is an occasion for beginning with God. Every joy and success is an occasion for beginning with God. Every day is a day for beginning with God, every moment a moment for beginning with God. Every thought, every word, every act is an opportunity for beginning with God. When we allow all things to begin with God we shall see new beauty and truth, new wisdom and love, our world filled with radiance and glory, our self filled with the realization of our natural divinity and heritage of eternal joy.

Meditation for Self-Help

This is God's day. This is God's universe. The body I inhabit is God's holy temple. In Him I live and move and breathe and have my being. My Father and I are one.

All the thoughts I think are God's thoughts. All the words I speak are God's words. All the deeds I do are God's deeds. I am here to express Him every day of this life and forever after.

Every experience that comes to me is God's opportunity for more expression of Himself through me. I am required to do nothing "on my own"; for it is His wisdom and understanding, His love and peace, His joy and enthusiasm and inspiration that work through me to attain expression. I am God's radiant, progressive, successful child manifesting ever more and more of His glorious nature.

"Fear Not!"

IF SOMEONE were to ask me what I consider the most helpful in overcoming physical, mental, or bodily ills, I believe my answer would be, "The overcoming of fear concerning those ills." Fear, defined by Webster as the "painful emotion marked by alarm; dread; disquiet," is the basis for the prolongation of most difficulties experienced by man. Yet, because fear is an emotion, it is rightfully subject to man, not man to it.

A friend wrote recently, "I want so much to have faith and understanding, but I am fearful and I cannot seem to overcome the fear." My friend's situation is similar to that of thousands of others who are confronted with appearances of physical disturbances and negation. The first reaction to such appearances is dread of what they may mean, the focusing of the imagination upon what impending danger or evil they may bring. Right at this point we need to take a definite stand; we need to recognize the truth that we are children of God and, as such, we have been given dominion over all the earth according to His word and promise.

How do we go about taking this stand? The same way Paul did, by saying, "None of these things move me." The same way David did, by declaring, "In God have I put my trust, I will not be afraid." The same way Daniel did, by turning from the lion-like evidence to the light of Truth. The same way Job did, by searching with all his heart for the good within the very darkest of appearances. The same way the Master did, by declaring, "Get thee hence, Satan," and turning to the Father within.

You and I are no different from any of these individuals, for we are all children of the same God. We have no less authority than they had; we only need to claim our authority and practice outwardly our inner beliefs in a bolder fashion. If we need to tap our feet and speak aloud to ourselves to prove our belief and authority, then let us do so! If we need to sit in silence and pray more often than we have in the past, then let us do so. It is just such action that relegates fear to its native background of impotency! If we believe that fear has only the power we give it, then let us refuse it any place in our lives!

Think deeply about this for a moment. Why

do you suppose it was so simple for those who came to the Master to receive the desired healing? Was it not because, in His presence, they were no longer fearful of the claim of evil in their lives? Think for a moment what your attitude would be, if you had opportunity today to stand before Jesus. Would you not be filled with limitless love for this leader who proved His mastery through innumerable outer works? Would you not be instantly convinced that He had power to proclaim good for you?

Coming into His presence, you might be inclined to kneel with bowed head before the radiant light shining from His countenance. You would suddenly realize what He so surely knows—that the only power and presence in all the universe is God; that anything appearing to the contrary is of no importance, not real, and, therefore, not to be feared. Your fear of the condition or the problem would fall from you because of the overwhelming awareness of His love and His power.

Then, as you worshiped in silence and in thankfulness, perhaps He would quietly remind you that it is the Father within, not His personal self, that "doeth his works." He would tell you that you are a son of the Most High, possessing all the characteristics of the Christ nature, able to prove the same works and even greater ones. He would bid you arise out of the consciousness of disbelief with the words: "Fear not, only believe." "All things are possible to him that believeth." It would be impossible to fear anything—however frightening in appearance—before the light of such calm assurance and divine authority!

Now, dear friend, this light of assurance and authority can be ours today—through our inheritance of the Christ self. This light of dominion did not fade with the crucifixion of the man Jesus. It has, instead, grown brighter and stronger. Every trial of mental or physical negation in our lives is but another period of crucifixion, and we must remember the importance of the event following, the resurrection, and accept the truth that we, too, through our spiritual sonship, can arise to receive our rightful heritage of good. We must arise and proclaim daily this dominion of Christhood, which is inherently our own!

By thought and word and action we enforce this spiritual proclamation until our entire inner being accepts it for the truth it is, and perfection is manifested in our lives and affairs. It was no easier for Jesus to do this than for any other man, except that His earnestness and love were supreme. When you become as sincere as He, when you are as faithful as He, when you love the Lord your God with all your heart, with all your soul, with all your strength and mind and might as He, then you, too, move toward the expression of your Christ dominion. And as you begin walking in the right direction, through strong and positive thoughts and words and actions, you shall find all things about you moving in the same direction—toward your increasing good.

When my fearful friend who desired faith and understanding took the necessary stand of authority, refused to accept fear and its implications, and proclaimed her dominion as a child of the Most High, the appearances became unimportant and began to fade. It is always this way. When we proclaim by positive thought and word and action that which is Truth, the surrounding appearances of evil and terror and negation suddenly lose the power we have given them and fade into nothingness.

Perhaps something is troubling you at this time, something that has been persistent, obstinate, seemingly unresponsive to your declarations of Truth. If a negative condition harasses you, use a clear, strong, definite rebuke regarding its appearance of power. Don't ignore it or push it into the background of your mind. Rather, face it squarely, bring it to light, and say calmly but determinedly: "Be cast out! You are a liar. You came forth from nothing, you are nothing. You have no power of your own, and I will not lend power to you. Get out and stay out."

Each time the appearance makes itself known to you, arise and rebuke it with dignity, power, and spiritual authority as did Jesus. You have this same dominion over the elements, over the "demons" of humanness, that Jesus Himself possessed through the divine Sonship. You, too, are a son of the Living God. You, too, can command the undesirable to depart and be no more, even as Jesus set the example.

As you persist, as you are watchful and alert and continue in prayer, you will find that there arises within you a Christlike authority that makes known to you your innate ability to f low in Jesus' footsteps. You will realize that it is not by any human force the negation is dissolved, the good brought forth; but that by the all-powerful Spirit finding free expression through you the work is accomplished.

Each time you arise, each time you take this stand of Christlike dominion, blessings will follow. You will realize a great calm in your mind and heart concerning all false appearances, each time you let God work in and through you to bring forth good. You will find all demoniac trials hold nothing but gain and progress, that all feverish conditions promise nothing but purity and refreshment for the awakening of new spiritual values and material enrichment.

Even though it may seem that you can never attain true Christ mastery, even though the burden of fear seems to weigh as heavily as ever after you have put forth an effort to overcome it, do not give up. Refuse to give up! What if Peter, after his miserable failures at steadfastness and faith, had not continued trying? He did sink into the depths for a time, but he put forth another effort, tried again, went forward another step, and then found that which he sought—inner authority, spiritual dominion—

and thereby brought light to thousands along the way.

It is not a gay, carefree life devoid of all trial and difficulties that promotes and urges the accomplishment of the high goal. All the persons in the past who have brought light and inspiration to their fellow men have known darkness and terror along the road, and the very urgency and desperation of their struggles has been transformed into an uplifting force for their highest good. Those who have spoken the most inspirational words, written the most glorious themes have undergone the most discouraging temptations, the most disheartening experiences.

A friend once said, "It is this very fright and fear that have brought me the greatest faith and deepest understanding." When will you and I begin to awaken, so that we can say the same? Not because we must become like Jesus or David or Job or Paul, but because we *are* like them; because we are all children of God, one Father-Mother, Creator, and Sustainer of all; because we *already* have inherited the same spirit of courage and power, authority and discipline, the same capacity for limitless love.

Though the mountains tremble and be cast

into the sea, though the earth shake and crumble beneath our feet and before our eyes, let us not be moved, but rather stand fast on the firm ground of the truth that we are sons of God, created with power and authority and dominion from the very beginning!

Right now you are the steadfast and immovable and triumphant person you want to be! Right now you are the poised and calm and undisturbed person you desire to be! This is your heritage, dear one, not something to be put off until everything about your life and affairs is different. You are the one to take command, and through this very act will the outward appearances change from darkness to light. You are a splendid and triumphant and glorious child of God now! There is nothing in all the universe that will not respond to this exercise of dominion. Believe this and act upon this belief, and nothing can prevent your victorious overcoming! You are a son of God, strong and free in the power of His might!

Meditation for Self-Help

"Acquaint now thyself with him, and be at
    peace:
  Thereby good shall come unto thee."

  "Thou wilt keep *him* in perfect peace, *whose*
mind *is* stayed *on thee;* because he trusteth in
thee."

  "Peace I leave with you; my peace I give
unto you . . . Let not your heart be troubled,
neither let it be fearful."

  This same peace is now within you, beloved,
just as it was within our Lord Jesus Christ in
His earthly ministry. It now fills your spirit,
soul, and body with the calm and joy that
"passeth all understanding."

  It is the same landscape in a gossamer veil
of moonlight; the same peace that fills the hush
before the dawn, when all the world awaits in
silence the glory of the rising sun, come to bless
the earth with life and strength; peace that fills
the night with soft beauty, infolding the same
peace that flows across the broad, shining acres
of golden waving grain; the same peace that
whispers gentle notes of love among rustling
leaves in wooded dells; the same peace that

settles softly and gracefully with each perfectly formed snowflake; the same peace that twinkles silently across millions of miles from the myriad blue, red, and silver stars in the heavens; the peace that accompanies the perfect rhythm of the tide rising and falling on rocky beach and sandy shore; the peace that smiles from placid depths of quiet lakes, that flows with sureness and purpose as the rivers journey to meet the open sea, that glimmers in sparkling raindrops refreshing all living things.

All nature joins in the perfect, harmonious melody of peace that arises from true communion with the Creator, who made the world and pronounced it good. Listen to its quiet song of love! It fills all space and blesses all who hear! His peace, beloved, infolds you now, encompasses your every day, surrounds your loved ones, and blesses every situation, permeates your mind and body with the joyous radiant knowledge that God is in charge and all is well.

"Finally, brethren, whatsoever things are true, whatsoever things are honorable, whatsoever things are just, whatsoever things are pure, whatsoever things are lovely, whatsoever things are of good report; if there be any virtue, and if there be any praise, think on these things."

"And the peace of God, which passeth all understanding, shall guard your hearts and your thoughts in Christ Jesus."

Give Up to God

IF THERE IS a problem of health, supply, or harmony facing you, one you have tried steadfastly and sincerely to solve for some time without success, pray once more as the Master taught, then turn the whole burden over to God. Do this not in an attitude of discouragement and failure and weariness, but in an attitude of willingness to let go, to give up to God.

For many of us, personal pride and human willfulness stand in the way of progress, blocking and impending the easy acceptance of our heritage of All-Good. This was made startlingly clear to me during a prolonged time of inability to convince another of his spiritual birthright of happiness and peace. One morning, after earnest and humble prayer, a voice suddenly spoke strongly and clearly from within saying: "You have nothing, personally, to do with this! Forget yourself, forget this frustration and effort. Be willing to lean upon the One who giveth the increase, the Father, the One who doeth the work."

I knew then that my mistake had been dependence on human knowledge instead of on Spirit, on human effort rather than on the "zeal of Jehovah of hosts." This awakening marked the beginning of progress and understanding for all concerned. Many, many times since then this inner advice has been repeated when I have found myself becoming anxious or tense about a negative situation.

Fretting and stewing and conniving do not draw us closer to our good, to greater wholeness of body, illumination of mind, harmony of affairs. Such attitudes only delay and hinder the good results we seek, while willingness, co-operativeness, and expectation hasten our receiving of the blessings desired. When we add to this willingness and co-operativeness, faith in the infinitely wise Father, there is no limit to the good we may claim and receive.

Only when the personal, human self becomes willing in consciousness to "sit down in the lowest place," can the still small voice of God be heard saying: "Friend, go up higher: then shalt thou have glory in the presence of all that sit at meat with thee. For every one that exalteth himself shall be humbled; and he that humbleth himself shall be exalted." This is the direct and unmistakable advice of the wisest of all teachers as given in His parable concerning those who desired to be seated in the most honorable place at a marriage feast.

In this parable we can see what He wants us to understand, that only through our willingness to humble our worldly thought, to "sit down in the lowest place," can we find the real self, the Christ self, which is worthy of the highest place, the place where we can behold and receive the full glory and honor of our heritage.

How can humbling ourselves help us realize perfect health? By humbling every thought regarding man-made laws of physical health, by humbling human reasoning and argument, by humbling our consciousness before the Creator of perfect wholeness we permit the arising of the Christ self within, the self that knows but one source of perfection. As we become wholly meek and humble we neither condemn nor accuse nor argue concerning the appearance of things, but are simply ready to listen for the guidance of that inner real self which knows itself to be "greater . . . than he that is in the world."

If your problem now concerns health, let go of resistance to the appearance of ill-health, let go of all personal struggle and give up to God wholly and completely your whole being, your very life. You, humanly, have nothing to do with the creation and sustenance of this life. This is God's work, God's idea, and He will not fail to fulfill it according to His highest desire of good for you.

If your problem concerns success or attainment, let go of rebellion against obstacles and failure, let go of all personal striving and give up to God wholly and completely your deepest desires, your most heartfelt aspirations. You, humanly, have little to do with the development and fruition of your fondest dreams. This is God's work, His increase, and He will not fail to fulfill it.

Hourly we have opportunity to put into practice the rewarding spirit of willingness, and daily learning that willingness in small things will help to prevent the disease of willfulness in major situations. Willingness is interpreted to mean being "favorably disposed in mind." So we must, in day-by-day tasks and prayers, be "favorably disposed" in thought and heart toward God. We must let Him give the increase, while we watch and pray, doing all things lovingly and without reluctance.

No matter how rushed we feel, no matter how urgent any matter appears, and no matter how confused the issues of our life seem to be, let us take a few minutes right now to tell the Father: *"I rest in Thee. I wait for Thee. Thou shalt bring it to pass."* Let the whole body become relaxed. We can do this without anyone else's being aware of it, so we need not postpone it to some other time or place.

As we feel ourselves letting go of the tension, we repeat the affirmation either silently or aloud, slowly, calmly, and with faith, placing emphasis upon the words *rest, wait,* and *Thou.* As we repeat this procedure seven times, with a slight pause between each declaration, upon the seventh repetition, let us stop, be still, relax, and let go still more completely, clearing our mind of all thought activity. Let us just be still.

If we do this once, we shall find immediate release from the anxiety and tension that have plagued us. If we do it a second time, we shall find ourselves becoming more confident and assured and faith-filled. As we keep it up, exercising and practicing throughout the day in this manner, we shall find the whole attitude changed, the body eased of all tightness, and the entire aspect of the situation altered. Indeed,

"Thou shalt forget thy misery . . .
As waters that are passed away."

So it is, beloved friend, that as we admit our seeming failures and mistakes, become humble and willing as a "little one," we draw nearer in consciousness to the heavenly kingdom, nearer to the realization that God's will for us is one of beauty, joy, wisdom, and love. We begin to understand that in giving up our own personal will, in giving up to God, our ways are made straight and smooth, our burdens light, our paths joyous.

"Giving up to God" is not an attitude of subjection but of faith and courage. It means having faith in the Father who "doeth his works" and "giveth the increase." It means having courage to give up personal pride, limited selfish desires and beliefs, for the conviction that the divine will is a supreme design for good, for joyous attainment.

The Father has more happiness and peace

and love, greater fulfillment and satisfaction
for us, than we can imagine, but we must learn,
through humility, meekness, and willingness to
accept this treasure. Someone once said, "Man
would rather refuse the gifts of God than admit
his mistakes." Yes, beloved, we need to pray
daily as the Master taught, "forgive us our
debts," in order to humble the personal self
into quiet acceptance of Truth. The more humble we become, the more Christ power we find
within; the more meek we become, the greater
the life we discover within; the more ready we
become to give up to the divine will, the more
perfect the fulfillment of our greatest dreams
and desires.

Begin now, dear friend, to know "the God
of thy father, and serve him with a perfect heart
and with a willing mind." Begin now to give
up all insistence upon the attainment of your
goal according to your human plan. Give up all
to God and rest in the complete ease and peace
of willingness. The Father has a way you know
not of to show you the wonders of His love,
the joys of His perfect plan for you. Relax and
rejoice, child of God, for "the zeal of Jehovah
of hosts will perform this."

Meditation for Self-Help

When you have gone as hard as you can go all day long; when fears for loved ones have beset and harried you; when courage seems to have failed and all the worries of the day have crowded tensely into the nooks and crannies of your being; when you wonder how you can ever take another step, smile another smile, lend another helping hand—then take a moment to be still and listen for your Father's voice.

Sit quietly and relax every part of your body. Imagine a curtain of rich black velvet before your eyes; picture God's great Spirit of peace flowing through every muscle, every organ, every cell. *"Peace, peace."* Whisper it softly, lovingly, repeating it: *"Peace, peace. I am filled with whole, complete, and perfect peace. My eyes see peace, my ears hear peace, my lips speak peace, my whole being radiates infinite, omnipresent peace! From tip to toe I am the perfect expression of peace! It cleanses, heals, purifies, renews, and vitalizes me now. I am peace."*

Then let go and let God, and listen in perfect, receptive stillness for His voice. "The peace of God, which passeth all understanding," will be yours. I know; for I have done just this in the very midst of work at the office, after a crowded, hurried day, when angered by a disturbing situation, when fearful of the bigness of life, when frightened about the safety of a loved one. Declaring God's peace soothes mind and body, calms the spirit, and brings not only complete and wonderful peace, but a strength and courage unknown before.

"Peace I leave with you; my peace I give unto you."

"Thou wilt keep *him* in perfect peace, *whose* mind *is* stayed *on thee.*"

Perfect peace is yours. Take it, use it! It is God's gift to a beloved son, awaiting your acceptance. It is part of the Father's lavish and abundant love poured out upon those who are willing to receive, to use, and to give.

Simple Prayer

ERHAPS you are now saying: "Yes. I agree that I should relax and let go of the difficulty and let God do the work, but how am I going to be able to do this when outer difficulties press upon me and the need is so desperate, so urgent? How can I relax and let go, and pray easy as you say?"

Several years ago, while I was talking with a loved friend and Truth teacher, she mentioned that she seldom asked the Father for anything when in need, but, instead, used often the simple words, *"Father, I'm trusting!"*

She used them when she did her studying, as she went about helping others arise out of their difficulties, as she carried out her daily tasks and household duties, repeating the words either silently or aloud with calmness and assurance.

When I encountered a personal trial a short time after this, these words returned to me with new emphasis and meaning. When I repeated them in a quiet, but firm, manner, the burden was lifted and the problem solved. In other instances that followed, I again used this little prayer, and as a result a desired household article was supplied unexpectedly; I received as a gift two beautiful new suits; longed-for flowers for the yard materialized; an ink-spot came out of a dress after I had been told it could not be removed; an important telephone call was completed in spite of seeming obstacles; I was able to procure an automobile when none seemed available.

Perhaps you think your problems are more complicated and difficult and involved than mine, that you cannot accomplish the desired miracle of healing or harmony or supply with such a small and simple prayer. No matter what your problem, no matter how great or small its size, the Father never fails. But we must turn to Him in order to receive His blessing. This is what the little prayer, *"Father, I'm trusting!"* helps us to do. It turns us, our thought and attention, to Him, to the One who is the Source of all our good, the Creator of all good, the Father of our being.

Most of us rise above our difficulties through persistent small prayers rather than a single big soul-sweeping one. The turning of the moment is the important thing, and this turning of our attention to God, the all-powerful indwelling and ever-present God, is the way we find Him and the solution to our problem. The more often we turn to Him the more often we are consciously with Him, and the more we are consciously with Him the more like Him we consciously become, manifesting perfection in mind, body, and affairs.

There is nothing so deeply imbedded in your consciousness that it cannot be removed, whether it concerns a problem of health and wholeness, or supply, or human relations. As you begin to say, *"Father, I'm trusting!"* you begin your acquaintanceship with the Most High, and find Him very near, even within you, as the strength of your heart, the guidance you desire, and the light of inspiration.

This practice of speaking simple prayers does not mean that periods of silent prayer and meditation are not of great value and necessary, for no one can grow in spiritual stature and grace without such practice. But by holding to a small prayer such as *"Father, I'm trusting!"* throughout the day, we form the habit of consciously taking God into every moment of our day, becoming aware of His presence within every moment of our day.

A Truth teacher said recently, "When you begin to invest one hundred per cent of yourself in God, you will begin to find the one-hundred-per-cent returns you are looking for." When we begin to invest all of ourselves, one hundred per cent of our thoughts and words and actions, in God, the All-Good, we shall find that we express the fullness of God, and we shall find the truth and perfection of the kingdom coming into evidence in our life.

A young woman, down to her last dime, read the words "In God We Trust" inscribed on the small silver coin, and her renewed faith encouraged and enabled her to secure the position she so desperately needed. Hundreds of times before that moment the silver pieces had passed through her hands, the words unnoticed. How often the infinite treasures of God's kingdom pass us by unnoticed!

Our seeming inability to receive an answer to a prayer is many times due to our unwillingness to accept the answer that is simplest and most obvious. Perhaps, at other times, there seems to be no response to our prayer because we pray that the Father may give us exactly the kind of answer we want to receive. Perhaps we even tell Him the answer we desire Him to return to us as reassurance that our human deductions are correct. Or, perhaps in another instance, we tell Him how the situation must be handled, or we inform Him of the time element involved, or of what we think the other persons concerned must be made to do in order that the answer meet with our approval—as though we have forgotten that He is the author of infinite wisdom!

When a divinely simple answer comes that would have us renew or transform our own minds do we refuse to accept it as the true answer to our prayer because we would rather have other persons do the changing? When the "still small voice" speaks calmly within our hearts, telling us to be more patient, more trusting, to proceed with our day's activities in a spirit of thankfulness, do we overlook this inner counsel as the true answer to our prayer because of its simplicity? When the clear Truth concerning a condition we have prayed about dawns within our consciousness do we hesitate to accept it as the true answer to our prayer if

outer appearances continue for a time to belie
the spiritual revelation?

We want God's answer, but we oftentimes
hold to our own and thereby shut the door to
the good results that come from humble acceptance without question. As long as we are
fearful of what is spoken of in frightening
terms as "God's will," we are doubtful whether
God's will is good only! We wonder whether
He truly knows what is best for us, while we
ourselves are so sure of what is best from our
human standpoint!

If we acknowledge that God is our Creator,
a loving God, as Jesus taught, we can have no
qualms about accepting His will. If God is all
good, we can rest assured that His answer will
be all good, not part good and part bad. If God
is all wise, we can give up our human decisions
for His spiritual directions without reservation.
If God is all love, we can set aside our concern
for another's welfare and relax in the assurance
that nothing but good can result for our dear
one, regardless of what he seems to do humanly
to go astray from God's love.

God has a perfect answer for every one of
His children, for every one of their difficulties

in this life. He does not fail. His answer comes directly to you, from within your heart and mind rather than from someone else who advises or counsels you outwardly. Another person may be a channel for helping you find the answer to your prayer, but, still, the answer is your own, direct from God to you. No one else can know what this answer is. It is between you and God.

In the same way, you may not know the answer to your loved one's prayer. This, too, is a private matter between God and your loved one, and his answer will come to him at just the right time and in just the right way. There is never a delay in Spirit, and no answer will come too late. God is always on time, for He is ever present as well as all present.

A Truth student seeking an answer to a delicate problem in human relationships prayed earnestly about the matter. Although she felt that she knew the right step to take, she hesitated to create outer conflict. As she meditated upon the Father's love and wisdom and ever presence, the thought came to her, "Before the question arises the answer is there." Released from further anxiety, unburdened of personal responsibility, this Truth student knew that the right words would come forth, the right decision would be made for the good of all concerned. She had her answer and followed through in faith, and the results were manifested in harmony and order.

Long before the question confronting you arose within your heart the answer was there. Long before the earth was created and its creatures brought forth and man fashioned in the image and likeness of God, God was there in all His love and wisdom and goodness. He still is here, still in your life as your vitality, in your mind as your wisdom and good judgment and guidance, in your affairs as harmony and peace and order, happiness and perfection.

God has the answer to our problems, for He Himself is the answer to every heart's question or desire. He can answer the smallest, most trivial question, and He can answer the biggest, most serious, and complex question, for nothing is too difficult—or too easy—for God to solve. As the question arises within our hearts, so the answer speaks from within our hearts. The sooner we quiet the clamor of the human self, the demands of the personal, and become still and listen, patient and trusting, the sooner we hear and know the answer within our minds and hearts.

The Master, tried by every form of negation, confronted by questions and conflicts and doubts similar to ones that beset us today, found His answers through prayer, through turning within in faith, then moving outwardly step by step along the way. When He had prayed in faith He then acted in faith as though the answers already were, and the results were manifested accordingly. His persistence in so doing was not spasmodic or happenstance. He desired to persist in Truth and He continued to do so regardless of what others thought or said or did. His faith was not based upon outer results but upon inner conviction that came through prayer and the seeking of the Father's will of good.

He prayed and listened and found that the answers to the questions concerning sickness and unhappiness were wholeness and perfection and joy, the answers to the questions concerning sorrow and death were peace and happiness and life everlasting, the answers to the questions concerning problems of dissension and fear and hate were love and strength and courage. These answers arose within His heart, not from outer counsel and advice, and He went forth to carry out those answers in His words and actions in spite of the scoffing and disbelief of the surrounding multitude.

If your heart has called in anguish for an answer to grief or pain or lack, if your thoughts have been in torment over any difficulty concerning yourself or another, take time now to be still and pray once more. Know that the perfect answer you seek already dwells within your heart and is bringing forth the peace, assurance, and strength you seek, the same as it dwelt within the heart of Jesus and brought forth the peace, assurance, and strength that enabled Him to rise above all tribulation. Peace and satisfaction are your divine birthright as joint heir with the Christ. Be still and remember this, and remember that you were brought forth to be victor rather than vanquished, overcomer rather than the overcome. As you know this in the stillness of your own heart, a living answer will fire your being with renewed faith, cleanse you of the dross of unbelief and reveal the Truth. There is an answer, the Father's own to you, His beloved son!

Meditation for Self-Help

No matter what problem or difficulty you are facing today, God's answer is already on its way to you.

In the midst of inharmony or confusion, in the face of fear or grief, remind yourself that God's good, God's answer is already seeking you out.

God's help, which comes to us whenever we need it, may come through a friend, or it may come in the form of a stabilizing thought, a feeling of increased assurance, a renewal of courage. We do not always know what the channel for our blessing will be, or its method of reaching us, but we may be sure that the help we need in any given situation will reach us without delay.

God is the giver of all good. His blessings are never withheld but are poured out continually and abundantly upon us and our lives. Our part is to keep ourselves open and receptive to Him, to keep ourselves ready and willing to receive His good.

Whatever your need, whatever your desire —supply, health, happiness—it comes direct from the one source and it is made manifest for you as you keep your faith centered in God.

Are you hurt and unhappy about something or someone? Ask for God's help and then be ready to receive.

As you listen in the silence, you will receive God's answer; you will receive the uplift, the wisdom, the courage you need. You will find the peace and satisfaction you have longed for; your mind and heart will be filled with confidence. And even as you become an open channel for the blessings of God, you will become a channel of good for the blessing of others. You will become a channel for praise and love, you will become a special messenger to bring happiness and joy to God's children.

Remember always that there are blessings for you. Open the door of your heart to receive them. Declare every morning, *"God has blessings for me today!"* He has! Prove Him now and receive your very own good.

Act on Belief

IS IT HARD FOR YOU to "have faith" today? Is it harder today to be steadfast in faith than it was yesterday? If so, then be grateful rather than dismayed, for therein lies your reward. It exists even within that seeming inability to remain firm in absolute faith. The strong, steady light of unwavering faith of those whom you have seen surmount obstacles and overcome adverse conditions has grown within their hearts in the same way yours is growing within you now. They, too, have prayed not one prayer of faith, but many.

There are problems that try us all, to the very point of despair and heartbreak, and yet, it is at that point we can arise to our greatest conviction and most powerful authority as children of God. It is at that point we take another step forward into a steadier and more assured consciousness of the reality of good. The Father has not mocked His beloved heirs by placing within them a meager supply of faith, just enough to meet a few small trials, but has bestowed upon all a glorious and resurrecting faith more than sufficient to meet every need.

Whether it is the appearance of illness trying your faith in health, whether it is the appearance of lack trying your faith in abundance,
or the appearance of fear and inharmony trying
your faith in love, you have within yourself a
Spirit of faith greater than any physical appearance or any false belief or obstacle. The Father
has given you this faith, and has meant it for
good, has meant it for an active, living force of
good.

It is by positive action that our faith in God,
in good, develops and waxes strong. A friend,
sorely tried in many ways, wrote recently,
"There was a time when I thought it would be
impossible to make the trip to a government hos-
pital and undergo necessary examinations. I was
informed two weeks before the time to go and
immediately began to pray and to change my
fearful thinking into positive thoughts about
the matter. I was delighted and surprised too
at the way God gave me the power to overcome
fear and to have peace of mind throughout the
two weeks and during the trip. Now that I have
been retired and one phase of my life has been
changed, I'm sure another will start soon for

me—I can hardly wait to learn what it will be!"

This is faith! This is faith that is active, uniting heart and mind with its rightful inheritance of every good thing. This is faith that is being put to daily use. Are you thinking: "But I don't have that much faith. I wish I did—I wish I had more. I wish I had the courage to believe I can be healed (or prospered, or loved) but suppose I begin, and cannot finish—then I would have less faith than I have now!" Listen, beloved of God! The Father has not given you a spirit of fear or weakness or insufficiency but of power and love. All the content of His heavenly kingdom is to be claimed not by might but by faith, the kind we glimpse within the heart, then put into thought, word, and deed.

It is through daily exercise that our faith becomes stronger. It is by believing in the good we wish for, by daily and hourly expecting the good we hope for, by beginning to put that "wish" and that "hope" to active use, that we become more and more aware of the unlimited possibilities of faith.

Years ago, at a time when jobs were quite scarce, a young man was seeking a way to enter the business world. Although he was interested in Truth studies and knew the value of prayer, his attempts to apply the principles of prayer to his own life had not been successful. He finally voiced his difficulties to a lifelong friend: "How am I ever going to get a job? No one seems to want my services, and I don't know how to go about helping myself. What can I do?"

The older man looked at his young friend searchingly and replied simply: "Start your own business. You once told me of an idea you had for a business. Well—move a little. Take the first step. You said you wanted to sell electrical equipment. For that purpose you will need some kind of an office. Get yourself a room. It need not be an elaborate or expensive one. Then prepare yourself for selling."

This was the only advice the young man received, but as he walked down the street a few moments later, he found that he was stepping briskly in cadence with these thoughts: "Get yourself a room. Move a little. Take the first step."

Within a few days he had secured an office, which was small, but in a respectable location. Within a few more days he had ordered some business cards. For a time the office remained quite empty, but gradually it took the form of a progressive place of business. Phone, desk, and chairs were added, along with files and other needed equipment. Sales began to come in as he faithfully and zealously made the rounds, described his equipment to potential customers, and handed out his business cards. Within less than a year there was a large amount of electrical equipment being handled through this office, and there was an eager clientele ready to purchase. The young man had also acquired a partner to share in his growing sales work.

Many years later this person, then a successful businessman, remarked: "It was the simple suggestion of my friend that helped me to understand there was more to co-operating with God than 'just sitting and praying.' I knew then that I had to 'move a little,' as well as pray a lot. I had to move my feet in the direction I wanted to go."

If you desire to attain some high goal, to express some talent, or to enter some purposeful activity, set your mind and heart in its direction, pray, and then "move your feet" accordingly. Do not feel that your beginning step need be one that will claim great attention. The begin-

ning step need only be a simple way of show-
ing the Father that you believe in His kingdom
and His promises, that you believe in your divine sonship and inheritance of good.

Day by day take the steps at hand. Know
that with each step and each bit of guidance received there is steady progress toward the attainment of the good you are seeking. If at times
it seems that some of your activities are unre-
lated to your highest dream, only persist the
more diligently in following through to the best
of your ability; you will then see the value of
every effort and you will see the harmonious pattern gradually coming into manifestation.

It takes inner faith and outer application of
our faith to attain our goals and to reach the
high point of fruition in our lives, work, and
affairs. We have our portion to do, and God has
His. In order to do our share we must move in
the best way we can for the moment, for God
is ever moving in His best way for our highest
good. The more joyously we enter into this co-
operative process, the more easily, happily, and
successfully we will complete each step of our
journey toward perfection.

If someone we know well were to relate to

us one wonderful experience after another of
healing, of supply evidenced in their life through
faith, if he were to tell us of the marvelous
works faith had wrought for him in *this* day, it
might mean more to us than if we read story
after story of healing and blessing in Jesus'
time. It would bring home to us the truth that
faith knows no favored time nor age, but is as
powerful a force today as it was two thousand
years ago, and as it yet will be two thousand
years hence.

And yet, it is not, as Job says, by the "hearing of the ear" that our faith becomes strong,
but when we can say "now mine eye seeth thee,"
when we can "see" within our heart what faith
means to us personally, when we can feel its
power and presence within our own life experience, when it becomes to us a living word
whose whisper rises above and silences every
clamoring doubt and fear.

The most frequent advice of the Master
given to those who came to Him for healing
and help, was simply: "Believe!" "Have faith!"
Why? Because faith is the basis for the fulfillment of every good thing in our life. Faith in
perfect well-being is the basis, the substance, of

all health. Faith in abundance is the basis, the substance, of all supply. Faith in harmony is the basis, the substance, of all love. It is the basis of all the "greater *works*" the Way-Shower has told us we are to do today.

Many persons, long ago, thought they sought a man named Jesus, a man with extraordinary gifts of healing and blessing, someone who could offer them freedom and liberation from their fears and ills. But they actually sought, and within their inmost being they desired for themselves, communion with the Christ Spirit, which the man Jesus exemplified, a oneness with the spiritual nature He portrayed. It is the same with us today. There may be two thousand calendar years between the seekers of old and ourselves, but the inner needs are the same, the spiritual desires are the same, and the kingdom and its laws remain unchanged.

You and I need to turn within, acknowledge and put to use the faith already within our hearts, in order that we may begin to behold with the "inner eye" the wonders of our individual heritage of a living faith. That is what faith is, the movement of the inner longing for good into living action, thought, word, and deed.

Whatever your need of this moment, for health, strength, courage, supply, happiness— whatever it may be—within you, not within someone else you think more accomplished and gifted, dwells the vital life substance and power of all the good you can desire. Yes, you have within you all the faith you need for the perfect manifestation of any good thing. God did not promise that it is His good pleasure to give you the kingdom and then go back on His promise. He did not give you the inspiration of the life of His beloved Son, and then expect you to forget the wonders of that life.

Divine purpose lives behind that glorious promise, and divine purpose lives within the story of the Master's life. The Father intends for you and me to believe Him and follow through with that belief by putting it into our thoughts, words, and actions. He intends for you and me to walk in the footsteps of the Way-Shower and actively put to use the things we have been taught. He intends for us to realize that the faith within us is a dynamic faith of mighty works!

There is a divine design constantly at work each day. This divine design is co-operating with you unceasingly and inviting you to work with it to bring harmony into your life. Nothing is meaningless or futile in your life when Divine Mind works in and through every circumstance and every condition in your life.

If an endeavor is to become fruitful, there must be both spiritual and physical action. In your desire to go forward you must co-operate, or "move a little"; you must move more of your thought into prayer, a few more words into constructive speaking, and a few more steps into service. As you fulfill your part you permit God to fulfill His purpose in and through your mind, body, and affairs.

We need to seek no further for the step to take to achieve harmony and perfection in our lives. We need seek no pretentious way to follow, for Divine Mind is already stirring within us. Our part is simply to align heart, mind, hands, and feet with it! Our part is simply to "move a little" today in prayer; "move a little" in thought, word, and deed, and let God take care of the rest.

"Move a little," and you will find yourself within reach of your furthest goal; you will find the kingdom of heaven!

Meditation for Self-Help

As a child of God, confidence is my heritage, my true and natural state of mind. God created me in His own image and likeness and implanted a spirit of confidence within me, a spirit that believes in the outworking of good, a spirit that is sure of His ever-present, loving protection and guidance.

God is my help, and He is here now. In this I am confident. Despair is transformed into faith; darkness becomes light. I meet every situation and view every appearance with a fearless heart and a confident spirit.

I trust God for my abundant supply. I remember Jesus' admonition to His followers, "Be not anxious . . . if God doth so clothe the grass of the field . . . *shall he* not much more clothe you, O ye of little faith? . . . your heavenly Father knoweth that ye have need of all these things." I remember this promise and affirm: *"Father, You are my abundant supply. In this I am confident."*

I am confident that I am able to accomplish all things demanded of me. I am confident that God's wisdom in me is continually guiding and

inspiring me; I am confident that my capabil-
ities and talents have their source in Him. I am
confident that my every undertaking will be
attended by success, for the powerful and ac-
complishing Spirit of God is with me.

I am strengthened, renewed, and stabilized
as I express confidence in God, in myself, and in
my fellow men. God, all-good, is the only presence and power in my life and affairs and in the
universe.

As a child of the Most High, I have the authority to choose each day what I will serve. I
put my confidence in God and serve faith rather
than fear, happiness rather than unhappiness,
peace rather than confusion.

I take into my heart and mind a new confidence today, remembering that I am the beloved
of God, that I have not been given "a spirit of
fear but of power and of love and of a sound
mind." I remember that God's divine and perfect purpose for me is good, that He is with me,
as power and life, wherever I am and in whatever I do.

I remember that God has confidence in me,
that He created me in His own image and
placed His own Spirit within me, that He knows

all that I am capable of being and doing. God, in His infinite wisdom, has given me everything necessary for the perfect accomplishment of all the good desires of my heart. In this I am confident!

Speak the Word

IF YOU would demonstrate, attain, manifest greater good in your mind, body, and affairs, take time to speak aloud the word of Truth. Speak the word of wisdom, wholeness, harmony. Speak it aloud in the privacy of your own room or home until the air vibrates with the divine ideas contained within it!

If it is greater wisdom and understanding you desire, declare aloud, in a firm but gentle and confident manner: *"Let there be light. Let the clear light of God's day shine through my mind!"* If you are in need of healing, decree: *"Every cell of my body is indelibly stamped with a clear picture of radiant life. It now manifests that life!"* If you seem to lack any good thing, affirm, *"God is my unfailing, enduring, exhaustless supply."*

Do not strain or become tense or anxious in your speaking of these words, but repeat them in tones of peace, joy, and confidence, in the full awareness that it is the Father who does the work and brings forth the good results. Your part is to take hold of the divine idea in faith, speak the word in faith, and then in faith leave the outworking of that idea to God.

To help yourself realize the power of the divine idea indwelling in your spoken words, it is helpful to precede an affirmation with the thought: *"My words are Spirit, and they are life. They do not return unto me void, but prosper in the thing whereto I send them."* This affirmation reminds us that it is not really the words that we speak that are so important, but the spiritual idea contained within the words that is important. Knowing this truth also gives us a new feeling of strength and faith and conviction about our true words, their import and their miracle-producing activity.

As a certain Truth student prayed faithfully concerning her loved ones and gave thanks for the spiritual understanding she was receiving through a Truth teacher, she felt suddenly impelled to speak a word of thanksgiving and appreciation for that teacher. Suddenly she said aloud, "And, Father, an orchid to this good teacher!" She thought no more about her words until, during the next class session, she was startled into remembering her prayer when the teacher remarked, "It is always well for us to be open and receptive to our good because we never know just what nice surprise the Father has in store for us. This week He sent me an orchid through a completely surprising, unexpected channel."

Whether we understand that we are co-operating with the divine law or not, the law is constantly at work in our life. If we co-operate with it, putting our words to constructive use, we accordingly see the benefit of the constructive results that become manifest in our life. This is one of the basic teachings of Jesus: "Every idle word that men shall speak, they shall give account thereof. . . . For by thy words thou shalt be justified, and by thy words thou shalt be condemned."

Matthew, Mark, and Luke each give us the parable of "the sower" as taught by the Master, and each of them must have found this parable about sowing the word one of the most needful and important of Jesus' teachings. John, in his Gospel, also emphasizes the "word" and its importance, recording for us these statements of Jesus' "If ye abide in my word, *then* are ye truly my disciples." "If a man love me, he will keep my word." "If ye abide in me, and my words abide in you, ask whatsoever ye will, and it shall be done unto you."

If you find it difficult to assert your authority over the negative aspects of health, think more deeply upon the meaning of the beautiful name of Jesus Christ. This name is the symbol of all the health and strength and wholeness that any man anywhere can ever desire. It is in this name that healing power to raise the dead and give new life to the sick and the lame became manifest, and the command and authority of this name has not diminished. It is still filled with life-giving essence, with renewing breath and strength sufficient to open a new channel in us for God's perfect creation to flow into beautiful manifestation in our body, mind, and affairs.

There is not one among all mankind who has not received the gift of authority over all the earth, given him by the Father-Creator in the beginning. This gift is meant to be claimed and used as Jesus claimed and used it, to the glory of God and the upliftment of man and all other creation. Jesus, in telling us to follow Him, to do as He did throughout His earthly life, wants us to discipline our thoughts and our words so that we, too, can say with Him: "I and the

Father are one"; "I speak the things which I have seen with *my* Father"; "I know him, and keep his word."

Some time ago, this became clear to a Truth student as she sought her way out of financial difficulty. After working through prayer about her four vacant rooms, long unfilled by roomers, she suddenly awakened to the realization that Jesus spoke not only to man presenting himself for healing but to nature's elements and creations when He found it needful. Caught by the idea of the authority given every son of God, she decreed in new firmness and conviction: *"It is right for these rooms to be filled with fine roomers. I declare this house be put into useful service to mankind now!"*

She explained to a Truth counselor later that when she spoke the words in a tone of joyful command and thanksgiving she added emphasis to them by firmly striking the palm of her hand against the top of a table, deliberately impressing herself with the words through each physical action of her hand.

She added: "Also, whenever a thought of fear or doubt would return to me, I quickly stamped my foot and said, 'Get out of here,' in a firm and decisive manner, and then again claimed the good I knew was my divine heritage. Each of these simple little outer actions helped me not only to gain the attention of my thoughts but also to control them more effectively."

After placing an advertisement in the local newspaper for two days all four rooms were rented. This was three days after she declared her conviction through her spoken word and at a time many landlords were complaining about having vacancies.

Sometimes a student will protest, "But I have spoken the word of Truth concerning this situation, and nothing has changed." If we are faithful and persistent in speaking the true word, the change will become manifest.

Let us ask ourselves, "Has there been a constant, one-pointed direction of our mind to this truth?" Many times when we pray we declare in positive and emphatic words the Truth we desire to see manifested, and then, later on, throughout the day, express equally emphatic words exemplifying doubt, fear, and misgiving. It is for this reason that we need to repeat an affirmation again and again when we are experiencing a challenge or when we are facing an undesirable appearance. We need to repeat it until the Truth it expresses is firmly rooted and grounded in the very depths of our soul, and no evidence to the contrary can move it.

Jesus needed merely to say, "Go thy way; as thou hast believed, *so* be it done unto thee," when the centurion requested that his servant be healed. He needed merely to say, "I will; be thou made clean," to the leper; "Arise, and take up thy bed, and go unto thy house," to the palsied; "According to your faith be it done unto you," to the two blind men. He did not need to repeat and repeat and repeat the words over and over again, for the reason that the Truth had been established within Him—and it had been established not haphazardly or carelessly, but through endless days and nights of prayer and silence when He must have decreed again and again the truths His Father is so ready to share with all His children who will take time to listen—and then speak as He speaks!

If we find it necessary to speak the word of strength twice before it is manifest, that is all that is needful. But if we find it necessary to speak it twenty times, or two hundred times, or two thousand times, then we must be willing to speak it until that truth is immovable and solid and firm within the depths of our soul, our mind is steeped with it, our body temple is vibrant with it, our life is literally charged with it. Through our persistence in looking away from the appearance, through our constancy in looking within to the Truth, through our faithful and steadfast thinking, speaking, and acting in accordance with the Truth, the Truth finds freedom of expression through us.

A young girl, particularly desiring to attract right companions, took into her heart the affirmation, *"I am magnetic with the irresistible charm of Spirit."* Within a week she was blessed in having an unusual number of happy social times and met several fine new friends. Her mother, a good Truth student, remarked later, "The thing that impressed me about Jane's attitude was the feeling she put into her efforts. When she declared this truth for herself, she brought to bear on it all the faith and love and feeling she could muster."

Through years of habit many of us have unknowingly given great feeling to the negative aspects of life, even to the point of dramatically describing and enlarging upon them. All this must be done away with if we are to demonstrate the life abundant of which Jesus spoke. *All* our feeling, *all* our attention, *all* our devotion, *all* our interest must be directed to the divine idea we desire to be manifest!

Not in a spirit of driving, but in a spirit of gently leading, our thoughts, we can, moment by moment, day by day, acquire the spiritual habit of thinking and speaking we are intended to. Through a spirit of love, love for the goodness and beauty and truth of God and His kingdom, love for the joy and simplicity and perfection of Jesus' teachings, we can gradually walk more and more in paths of light and understanding, move more and more into active participation with God's law, reap increasingly more abundantly the blessings that follow.

In the beginning of our effort to overcome and be victorious we often have difficulty in affirming wisdom, or life, or success. Each of these goals seems unattainable, far beyond our reach, however desperately we desire it within our heart. Sometimes almost mechanically and automatically we begin repeating such words

as *"God is my life"* or *"God is my supply"* or
"God is my light." Yet, even as we begin, in
faith, to take hold of these divine ideas, something within us—that spirit of understanding
implanted in us by the loving Father—begins to
awaken, and there is a response. Sometimes we
do not recognize the response, but it is there,
and as we persist in our affirmations our consciousness is awakened to the basic Truth contained within the words we have spoken. As we
further persist in steadfast faith, more and more
love and deep feeling enter into our affirmations
until the very words are permeated with Spirit
life.

When we hear speakers give voice to words
of Truth, as we listen we perhaps feel that Spirit
life is expressed more fully through some words
than through others. Such awareness is simply
an indication of the extent to which the individual accepts the activity of Spirit within him.
As you and I let more and more of God or
Spirit move in and through us, through our
prayers, our words, the more vitally alive and
effective our words become until, like Jesus,
we need only to "say the word" and the good is
made manifest.

As we learn to become spiritually discern-
ing, spiritually watchful of all we speak as well
as think, we learn to choose words as Jesus Himself chose them and utter only right words,
good words, constructive words, spiritual
words, perfect words. Filling our minds, our
mouths, our hearts, with words of Truth, we find
our lives and affairs also filled with Truth. We
then find ourselves becoming the word of Truth
made manifest even as Jesus was "the Word"
made manifest, visible flesh.

Putting aside all words we do not desire,
choosing wisely all words we do desire, loving
these words, speaking these words, hearing them
with the inner ear, expressing them in speech
and activity, we shall rejoice in the wonder of
knowing how to co-operate with our Father in
order that He may manifest Himself to us, in us,
and through us. Realizing it is always the Father
abiding within us that does His work, we shall
speak the word with great humility as well as
calm command, with great thankfulness and expectation of limitless accomplishment. We shall
express our God through letting Him alone
speak through us. We shall be His Word made
flesh.

Meditation for Self-Help

I am free with the freedom of Christ. Through Christ within me I am free from bondage to any person, free from any situation that seems difficult, unhappy, or insurmountable. I am free from any condition that has been called incurable or pronounced impossible to correct. No matter how tightly human bonds and human beliefs have held me, I am no longer a prisoner. I declare in faith, "I am free with the freedom of Christ!"

I am unfettered and unbound; I am uplifted and blessed. I am free with the freedom of Christ. I need never run from a situation, avoid responsibility, or struggle to escape appearances, for my release is certain the moment I turn in consciousness to remembrance of the truth that I am a beloved son of a loving Father. Right where I am now, my freedom exists. Right where I stand now, God stands with me. Right here and now, my indwelling Christ is the victor and the overcomer.

I am free with the freedom of Christ. I accept the truth that within me is an indomitable self that is always unweighted, resilient, relaxed, and free. In Christ there is no burden of criticism, fear, worry, anger, resentment, envy, false pride, or any other negative thought. The Christ consciousness, which is my natural spiritual state, is not bound to undesirable habits, erroneous thinking, fearful imaginings. It is a consciousness of love, peace, poise, power, joy, and wisdom.

Jesus Christ has promised me rest from all labor and heavy burdens. He has promised me that His yoke is easy and light, and I believe His promise. I believe that as I follow His direction and believe in His words I shall find authority and dominion over all situations and conditions. Aligning myself with His ways and teachings, I find that I am unweighted, unbound, free with the freedom He taught.

If my daily work seems difficult, I take the advice of the Master and know the truth that sets me free, the truth that tells me I am free with the freedom of Christ. It is God who works with me and through me as my constant guide and instantly available resource. His wisdom, light, and understanding lift me up and out of all tediousness into easy accomplishment.

If I have assumed responsibility for the difficulties of a loved one, I affirm, *"There is only freedom in Christ."* I do not worry or grieve, either for myself or for another. I enter into the Christ consciousness of faith and trust. I turn to the silent place of prayer within my heart, knowing that God's will for me and for all is good.

If others appear to me to be doing the wrong thing or taking wrong action in matters of importance, I refuse to become anxious about results. I turn again to the thought, "I am free with the freedom of Christ," and reject the heaviness that accompanies human judgment and personal reasoning. I refrain from outer argument, even from well-meant suggestion. I release the situation. I establish myself in a consciousness of inner harmony, peace, and well-being, and I have faith that God's divine plan of good for all concerned is being brought forth.

My true Christ self is a joyous, peaceful, trusting self. This is the way I was created. I maintain the awareness of my true self by remembering that I am not a creature of burdens, weights, and fears, but a free and perfect child of the Most High. I remember that I am a child of peace, light, and faith, a child of love, courage, and wisdom. This is my heritage, and it contains no element of limitation or bondage. I accept this truth now and affirm it, believe it, speak it, and act it. Through Christ in me I am free, through Christ in me I am uplifted. Through Christ in me I am unfettered, triumphant, glorious, and free!

The Fruit of Patience

T HE YOUNG Truth student looked worried and fearful as she explained to the counselor the difficulty she was encountering. "If only Dad could see that by taking hold of an affirmation he could change his thoughts and attitude, I know that the physical condition would be immediately cleared up!"

The counselor looked at her lovingly and said: "I suppose a teacher hears those two words 'if only' more than any others. We are always placing a condition upon the manifestation of the good we desire, and it usually concerns the changing of another person. Don't be impatient about this, my friend. Have faith in him, in the Spirit dwelling within him."

The student broke in quickly: "But I have had patience! For the past year I've been praying about this, hoping he would do something that would be helpful. His eyesight is becoming worse; and if something isn't done soon, one way or another, it may be permanently and completely impaired!"

"My dear, we are told, 'He that believeth

shall not be in haste.' Your prayers have not
been in vain. Your father will find his perfect
guidance, but it will not be hastened through
any forcing on your part! If he doesn't accept
certain ideas you want to give him, don't force
them on him. Follow your own true inner direction about this. If you find opportunity, a time
when he is receptive, you might give him a
strong healing thought. But if this opportunity
is not presented, hold your peace and let your
patience have its perfect work. Then you will
see the reward of this patience in his life and
in yours as well."

Throughout the months that followed the
sincere young Truth student held fast to this
advice, turning again and again to the thought
and practice of patience—patience with herself,
patience with her loved one, and patience concerning the outcome she desired to see manifested. Occasionally she found opportunity to
offer her father a statement of healing and to
encourage him in the application of faith, but
most of the time she found that the simplest and
most harmonious way of giving was within her
own silent prayers.

She applied herself, with the continued guidance of the counselor, toward developing a patient attitude founded upon faith—faith in her own prayers, faith in her dear one's true spiritual inheritance of wisdom, faith in his spiritual heritage of the Christ indwelling, and faith in the Father for perfect outworking of the situation.

When her thoughts were drawn to the appearance of the condition, which at times apparently became more alarming, she deliberately turned away and spoke silently within her heart. Sometimes her words were, *"My faith works patience,"* or *"In quietness and confidence is my trust."* At other times she used the affirmation, *"The fruit of my patience is perfectness,"* or *"He that believeth shall not be in haste."* It took watchful self-discipline to refrain from speaking aloud the Truth principles that seemed to fill her heart to overflowing. It took constant self-discipline to turn her attention from the outer appearance and to hold to her faith in God's perfect work.

During the following year she found it necessary to travel to another state for her employer, but she remained faithful in her stand of patience, knowing deep within her heart that the Father's infinite wisdom and love would still watch over her dear one, that her own responsibility was merely her indwelling faith— faith in her own quiet prayer, faith in her loved one's true spiritual self, faith in the Father's wise outworking of the situation.

Six months passed before she returned home for a few days' vacation. As she sat with the family, which had gathered for an afternoon picnic, one of the children came to her for assistance in taking a cinder from his eye. She turned her attention to help him remove it and noticed her father standing close beside her, watching. As she was deftly and gently removing the tiny object, she heard her father speaking directly to her. He spoke in a low tone, but clearly and distinctly. "Well, there's nothing wrong with my eye!" Startled, she turned about for a moment and looked at him. She looked fully into his eyes from a level with her own and beheld immediately their clarity and physical perfection!

It had been almost four years since this Truth student began to turn her faith in the direction of prayer for healing of her loved one. In this period she had learned patience, self-discipline, steadfastness, and how to strengthen her faith. Now she beheld the fruit of her labor, the reward of her patience. She realized that her attitude of quietness and confidence, her restraint from forcing her ideas upon a loved one had helped him to believe and to find his own way of guidance toward healing and blessing.

Almost everyone, at some time, finds himself required to call upon patience in the outworking of a situation, condition, or appearance of difficulty in his life. There are times when we become impatient with ourselves or others, impatient with life's continuing trials and lessons, impatient because past efforts seem to produce little fruit, and impatient with the apparently small rewards of our long months or years of effort. For this reason Paul admonished his followers, "Let us not be weary in well-doing: for in due season we shall reap, if we faint not."

For this same reason, many of the Master's parables stress the importance of patience and steadfastness. When He spoke of the kingdom of heaven, likening it to a mustard seed, we find the words, "when it is grown," preceding the promise, "it is greater than the herbs, and becometh a tree." Speaking of this same kingdom in likening it to a fisherman's net, we find that the words, "when it was filled," precede the gathering of the good from the net.

In the parable of the talents we are reminded that it was the "faithful" (steadfast) servants who entered into the joy of the Lord. In the parable of the seed cast upon the earth we are reminded that the earth bears fruit with "first the blade, then the ear, then the full grain in the ear." In the parable of the sower we are reminded that "the word" within the honest and good heart must be held "fast" in order to "bring forth fruit with patience."

The very first declaration regarding the universe and all creation came direct from the Creator Himself, who called everything "good," and this is the divine pattern for every word of every kind to His children, now and forever. No matter from whom, or through whom this word must come, it will begin with the loving Father. No matter what needs to be brought about or arranged, what condition needs adjustment, what seems to be taking so long to become manifest, rest in the knowledge that God is at work preparing His good for you.

God is at work in the very place where He seems least active, and right there He will become manifest in His greatest glory! He is at work on the very condition that seems most troublesome, and right there He will perform mighty things and bring forth order. He is at work in our very soul, where there seems to exist both good and evil, and right there He will show us our Christ Spirit, which is pure and perfect and radiant according to His idea for His beloved.

Not a moment too late does God provide, help, and save. Not a moment too late do we receive our guidance when we listen, watch, and pray. Not a moment too late do we receive our strength, courage, and renewed faith when we take firm hold of Truth. Not a moment too late will outer changes be effected when we are still and remember that God is always with us.

Perhaps you will say that this may be true in some cases but that it has not been true for you. You may feel that God has not helped you, that you have waited and waited and waited in vain for the assistance that you dearly desired and needed but that it has never come. If this is your thought, look to the reason for the delay. There is always a reason beyond that which appears to be an unanswered prayer or a so-called unheeded cry for help.

God is ever willing to help, to lift, and to rescue us from any situation. It is we who are not always ready and willing to be helped. Perhaps you will say: "You mean I don't want to be delivered from this state of ill health, lack, or inharmony? You can't tell me that. My constant prayer is for help."

Remember that there are always two involved in the process of a rescue: the rescuer and the one who is to be rescued. There must be co-ordination between the two. If we will look impersonally for a few moments at our attitude toward our healing, whether it is the physical, emotional, or financial state of our being, perhaps we will see why the rescue has not been concluded to our satisfaction.

If you find yourself discouraged today, dear friend, and tempted to give up because you feel you have been patient to the limit of your endurance, reconsider the words of the Master. Remember that "he that believeth shall not be in haste," regardless of whether the time has been four weeks, four months, or four years.

It is very possible that this week, as you determine to hold fast to your faith and patience, your reward will begin to be manifested. It is possible that this is the month the fruit of your labors will be harvested!

Jesus knew that many would rejoice to hear the promises of the Father that He came to earth to impart. But He knew, too, that His followers had to be deeply impressed with the importance of patience and steadfastness in the fulfilling of the desires of their hearts. He knew that their enthusiasm would reach its peak as He spoke of the kingdom and of man's divine heritage; but He knew also that human discouragement and impatience would dim their vision and slacken their pace.

In order to prove to us the value of every assignment, the gain of each lesson in our ongoing, Jesus unhesitatingly moved through every outer difficulty without resistance or impatience, teaching patience as He proved its value, speaking steadfastness as He also proved its value, until finally He had completed His mission on earth. He never sidestepped the obstacles in impatience. He never rode hastily or roughshod over His assignments. He gained from them only greater spiritual maturity, bringing to light even more and more clearly the beauty of man's divine sonship.

All the fullness of perfect and eternal life, love, joy, and wisdom awaits every child of God. But this fruit becomes evident and tangible only when we are willing to prove ourselves patient, ready to count it for joy rather than disappointment and discouragement. It is within this challenge that the seed of the fruit lies dormant; and it is within our faith and patience that it is brought into maturity as a tangible blessing.

Take heart, dear friend, and know that your patience and steadfastness of the past, your renewed faith and patience of this day are now bringing you into a new awareness of a life of abundance, a fullness of joy, a message of overcoming and victory given by the Master. Continue in this patience and steadfast faith. You shall find that the harvest is great, that the fruit of the Spirit will overflow into your life in a measure infinitely more abundant than you have ever dreamed. "Let patience have *its* perfect work, that ye may be perfect and entire, lacking in nothing."

Meditation for Self-Help

God's perfect action is moving in and through you, in and through every circumstance of your life. Remember this when your progress seems slow, when your financial affairs seem confused, when you are tempted to doubt and fear concerning a move to be made, a stand to be taken.

God's action is always wise and loving. It is constantly moving throughout creation, a harmonizing, healing power. Without force, without strain, it moves to bless, to lift, to bring forth good. It moves through your mind to illumine you, to inspire you, to enlighten you.

The right action of God now moves through your body to harmonize, to heal, and to strengthen you. The right action of God now moves through your heart to uplift, to cleanse, and to purify you. The right action of God now moves through your life to prosper, to satisfy, and to bless you.

If you seek guidance and direction at this time, realize that the perfect action of the One who made the heavens and the earth now moves through your thoughts, gathering them together in spiritual order and strength, developing your true purpose, clarifying your vision. Affirm, *"The perfect action of God directs every thought I think, every move I make, and all is well."*

If your need is for greater realization of wholeness, remember that God's perfect activity is the great equalizer of every bodily function, the great harmonizer of every feeling and emotion. Let go of tension and anxiety through letting go of personal striving, through remembering that it is the Father within who does the work. Repeat lovingly, *"The Spirit of God is active within me, promoting order, harmony, and healing."*

There is no place where the activity of God is not present. There is no situation in which the activity of God is not in command, in which the activity of God is not at work. As the Spirit of success, God moves through every financial understanding, through every business venture, through every transaction. His action is never delayed; it always brings about a perfect solution and joyous progress. Affirm, *"God's perfect action directs my efforts, guides my desires, and prospers my endeavors."*

There is no haste in the activity of God. If you feel pressed by circumstances, pushed by events, spend a few moments contemplating God's action within His universe. Picture in your mind's eye the quiet, orderly movement of the stars and planets across the heavens. There is no hurry, no confusion, no uncertainty here. God's activity always is one of peace and order, and when we remember this it is reflected in our own lives, and our affairs are blessed accordingly.

The perfect action of God illumines and inspires you; it moves through your body as renewed life, through your affairs as abundant success. You are a radiant channel, overflowing with the perfect activity of God!

What Do You Make of It?

A TRUTH student was severely criticized and condemned by a woman who misunderstood the facts involved in a situation. When the student was told of the criticism, something within her seemed to say quietly, "Well, what are you going to make of it?" Her first thought was of the injustice of the condemnation and of finding some way to explain the situation to the woman. Her second thought, as she turned to Spirit for guidance, was: "Truth needs no defense. My business is not to attempt to justify myself to man, but to follow the Christ teachings and be true to God."

After speaking a word of forgiveness in silent prayer, she set about turning the incident to good by declaring that it would bring to her only greater faith, greater compassion, greater understanding, a greater degree of love than ever before. As she prayed about the problem she felt as though she were infolded in a gentle atmosphere of love, that every hurt feeling was transmuted into a new awareness of love for God and all mankind.

Within a few days the Truth student received an unexpected telephone call from the woman for whom she had been praying. During the conversation, as they exchanged kind and friendly words, the misunderstanding and tension gave way to understanding and peace, and harmony was restored between the two women. Through this experience the Truth student found that by refusing to make something of the incident, and instead making the most of God the good, she received a deep blessing of new spiritual understanding, a blessing that not only benefited herself, but also benefited everyone connected with the situation.

Sometimes our difficulties seem greater than we can bear, and because of them we become easily led into a state of resentment and rebellion. Such attitudes of mind do nothing to help the situation. They only bring us down lower and lower into further and deeper discouragement. To help ourselves out of such a negative state of thinking and feeling, we need to take some strong and definite stand; we need to make some definite personal effort, clear-cut enough that the negative thought will be routed from our conscious and subconscious mind.

It is necessary that we be firm and authoritative at such times, as firm and authoritative as Jesus was when He rebuked outer rebellious appearances in order to open the way for perfect healing and blessing for His followers. At one point, you will remember, in the case of the man with the unclean spirit, as related by Mark, "Jesus rebuked him [the unclean spirit], saying, Hold thy peace, and come out of him. And the unclean spirit . . . came out of him." In another instance, when Simon's wife's mother was "holden with a great fever . . . he stood over her, and rebuked the fever; and it left her: and immediately she rose up and ministered unto them."

In still another instance, when Jesus was with the disciples, "they reasoned one with another" concerning an appearance of lack and they received His deep rebuke. He charged them quickly and sternly: "Why reason ye, because ye have no bread? do ye not yet perceive, neither understand? have ye your heart hardened? Having eyes, see ye not? and having ears, hear ye not? and do ye not remember? When I brake the five loaves among the five thousand, how many baskets full of broken pieces took ye up?

And when the seven among the four thousand, how many basketfuls of broken pieces took ye up? . . . Do ye not yet understand?"

The disciples must have been quickly silenced and ashamed for their having looked to appearances. Jesus' rebuke was intended to bring forcibly to their attention the Christ way of judging every situation: "Judge not according to appearance, but judge righteous judgment." This message is carried down through two thousand years for your benefit and mine today, to remind us to turn aside from all that appears to be, from the lack, the inharmony, the sickness, the unhappiness, and to turn, instead, to spiritual vision, to righteous judgment.

You may protest, "But it is hard to judge rightly when these negative things are right in front of me all the time!" It may, indeed, seem hard, perhaps foolish, sometimes even impossible to the reasoning mind for it to see wholeness where sickness appears, to see abundance where lack presents itself, to see harmony and love where unhappiness and inharmony seem to dominate. Yet this teaching, "Judge not according to appearance," is the key to the solution of any problem, the path to success and victory. This is the teaching of the Christ, His way of working with God, as taught by Him and lived by Him and proved by Him.

Whatever you seek today, be it the healing of a physical condition, the supplying of some great need in your life, judge not according to the appearance but judge righteous judgment. Judge as Jesus judged, not according to what the flesh presents, the situation reveals, the condition manifests, but according to Spirit and Truth!

Do you feel that such is too hard for you, even though others may be able to do it? Cast out the doubt! You can do it, or Jesus, your Teacher, would not have told you to do it. Say to yourself right now: "I will not judge according to the appearance. I will judge according to Christ judgment, the Truth!" You can do it. You can keep on turning away from every adverse indication simply by refusing to look at it, think about it, or speak of it, and insisting that the Truth be made manifest. You can!

It may take a dozen "turnings" within an hour, turnings from appearances of the physical senses to Truth as taught by the Master. It may take weeks of "turnings" each month, a hundred "turnings" of your mind and heart from the difficulty to God, from negative claims to spiritual truths. It may take a thousand declarations: *"I don't believe it. Only God, the good, is true!"*

Sometimes you may become extremely weary in your determination. Sometimes you may become tired and discouraged, ready to give up. Every overcomer has had his dark moments, even Jesus. His followers felt discouraged and ready to give up even when His ever-presence was at hand to help them. Remember that you have the same divine inheritance as the Master, and that He is backing you up in your ongoing and in your decision to judge according to Truth. All the powers of good in heaven and on earth will come to your assistance if you will take your stand and determine to accept the Christ reality only.

We may make something or nothing of the unwanted appearance in our mind, body, or affairs. We may make it something increasingly difficult to handle, something that possesses our every waking thought, governing and commanding us, or we may make it "as nothing," as the mist of the night that disappears with the dawn, simply a steppingstone to our greater good, an increase of our faith and understanding, simply a servant actually helping us into greater exercise of our spiritual authority and dominion over all the earth.

When Jesus rebuked the unclean spirit and it "came out" of the man, the bystanders were amazed, saying among themselves, "What is this? a new teaching! with authority he commandeth even the unclean spirits, and they obey him." No one before Jesus had exercised such spiritual command! The people had let themselves become overwhelmed by everything on the outside, by the "wind and the sea" of sense consciousness. It took the Master of life, Jesus the Christ, to show them the kind of attitude that quiets such storms and brings forth the "great calm" meant to reign throughout man's domain.

You and I, today, have the same claim to authority and command within ourselves that Jesus had. We are meant to call it forth and to exercise it through acceptance of our spiritual birthright and divine sonship. We either make something of the negative appearance or we make nothing of it through our spiritual rebuke and acceptance of the one presence and power, God the good. We either let it rule us, or we, ourselves, rule by the Spirit indwelling in us.

A woman found herself suddenly without an income, her position abolished when her employer entered another line of activity. When she went to a Truth teacher for spiritual help, the teacher said: "Let us make nothing of the appearance. Let us simply rejoice that another door has already opened to you." Losing only one day's work, the student stepped into another position easily and happily.

In another instance, a young man found himself severely tried by a claim of physical illness. When he called upon his friend, a Truth teacher, the friend urged him to declare: *"This appearance is a liar and the father of it. Only God is in me!"* Day by day, whenever insistent pain called his attention to his difficulty he sharply rebuked all fear and doubt and declared: *"Get out of here! God is at work! Only God is in me!"* This practice required persistent denial, persistence in turning every seeming obstacle to good, but within the year the victory was won. The young man declared later: "This problem of illness actually forced me into deeper spiritual understanding. In the beginning it seemed an obstacle, but now I see it as a blessing, a steppingstone into my greater good."

Someone may ask, "Do you mean that everything in our lives can be turned to good, no matter how disagreeable, difficult, or tragic the situation may be?" Yes! Everything, irrespective of its appearance or seeming negative nature, can be turned to good, transmuted into a blessing, in accordance with our attitude toward it. This transmutation involves a change in our consciousness, a transferring of our attention from negation to God, until we behold only God, only good, and nothing but good.

Whatever appears to hinder your progress into wholeness and life and strength may be the very steppingstone upon which you walk into complete renewal and awareness of life abundant. Whatever appears to impede your progress into success and happiness may be the strong foundation upon which you may stand still and see the salvation of the Lord. Whatever appears to retard your attainment of your desire may be the very vehicle upon which you ride into even greater satisfaction and fulfillment of your dreams.

Ask yourself now, "What am I going to make of this situation confronting me?" Are you going to let yourself be pulled down into it, or are you going to take inner Christ command and, as the palsied man was urged to do, "take up thy bed, and walk," that is, take up your thoughts and walk on into the consciousness of good prepared for you? The choice is up to you.

As long as you magnify the negation and hold onto it, tolerate it, feed it with your thought substance, it will be with you and be brought into continual fruition throughout your life. The moment you rise up in your innate spiritual authority and rebuke the appearance, it begins to recede and disappear from your life.

Instead of feeling our difficulties so deeply and dramatizing them, we need to turn from them and feel God more. Instead of magnifying and stirring up our human emotions over our human difficulties, we need to "stir up the gift of God" within us more faithfully than ever before. Instead of dwelling so devotedly upon thoughts and words of doubt and limitation, we need to "let the word of Christ" dwell in us richly, abundantly, hourly and momently.

Christ, the Lord and Master of your being,

indwells in you. Through Him you have absolute dominion over all that pertains to your life and circumstances. Take hold of your innate Christ authority and command today, and rebuke the undesirable thought, word, deed, condition, or circumstance that seems to hold you in bondage. Command the old false concept and negative thought, *"Hold your peace. God is all there is!"* Command the old false belief, *"Get thee behind me. My attention is centered on God!"* Command the outer appearance, *"Get out of here. The only power is God!"* Command the outer situation, *"Be cast out. Love prevails!"*

"With authority he commandeth even the unclean spirits, and they obey him." Such is your authority, as a child of the living God. Such is your command, if you will recognize and accept it. You are a child of the living God. You are not meant to be a servant of trouble, adversity, and sorrow. You are meant to be master of all life and being. This is your heritage of mastery, authority, dominion, through which you lay claim to peace, joy, and life abundant.

Take hold of your indwelling Christ authority now, and rebuke the negative thought that has been insisting upon attention. Declare its nothingness. Affirm that in reality it is a steppingstone upon which you will stand and rise into greater wisdom and light and understanding. Rebuke that ill feeling and emotion, and declare its nothingness! Affirm it to be in reality another opportunity to accept a greater measure of your spiritual heritage of joy and love and happiness. Rebuke that evidence of failure and declare its nothingness. Affirm it to be in reality good, an open doorway in a new consciousness of your indwelling spirit of success and accomplishment.

Rise up now, dear friend, and take command through the Christ indwelling in you. Take command through a rebuke of the appearance and repeat with the Psalmist,
"Jehovah saith unto my Lord,
 Sit thou at my right hand,
 Until I make thine enemies thy footstool.
 Jehovah will send forth the rod of thy strength
     out of Zion:
 Rule thou in the midst of thine enemies."

Meditation for Self-Help

If you feel that you are under criticism for mistakes of the past, take hold of the thought, *"The Christ in me is always worthy."* Let your faith in yourself find renewal in the knowledge that the Christ in you is ever worthy of the confidence of both God and man. Then you will dwell in strength and serenity and be filled with confidence born of Spirit.

This kind of confidence is based on spiritual truth, the truth that God the Father has implanted in you His own nature, His own life, intelligence, power, love, joy, and peace. This divinity within you is God's gift to you. It is unchanging, imperishable, eternal.

When we understand that we are children of God, the spiritual image and likeness of our heavenly Father, we are not moved by appearances, conditions, or personalities. Our reliance is on the Christ indwelling, on God within us, on God in everyone. *"The Christ in me is worthy. I give my best, and I am deserving of the best in return."*

This is a day for you to take new heart, a day to hold up your head, to straighten your shoulders, and to go forward in renewed faith. This is a day to know that you are the beloved of God, worthy of the very best.

You are worthy of God's faith in you, His trust in you. You are worthy of being called a child of God. God's opinion of you, His child, remains the same yesterday, today, and forever. The Father beholds you as His worthy child and heir, and the moment you turn to Him for guidance and strength He infolds you in tender compassion.

You are worthy of another chance, no matter how many times you seem to have failed before. The prodigal son made many mistakes, but his father found him worthy of the best.

The Father loves you unfailingly. Remember this throughout this day. You are worthy of your spiritual inheritance of wisdom, wholeness, and abundant good. God has faith in you. You are the beloved of His heart. Through the Christ in you you are worthy, deserving of the highest confidence of both God and man.

Only Good Can Come

HER EYES SHINING with a bright inner light that radiated peace and happiness, a Truth student came to me recently, saying quietly, "I've learned another great lesson through the Unity teachings, and wish to express my appreciation by telling you a bit of the experience, if I may."

Seeing my interest, she sat down for a few moments and related very simply:

"During a recent personal experience concerning human relationships, I found myself filled with confusion, doubt, and fear and I wondered why such a trial had come into my life. During this time I held the thought, *'It is only for good.'* I did not know what the outcome would be. I did not know the reason for the happening. I could not see any good in the condition. I could not see how it could benefit anyone concerned. All I could do was go forward in faith step by step each day.

"Every day I held to the words: *'It is only for good. Only good can come. All there is is God. All there is in this is God and God's good. Only* good fills this experience. Only good can come.'

"Upon awaking in the middle of the night, sometimes I walked the floor repeating these words, simply to keep out the doubts that besieged me. Sometimes I sat through the evenings in darkness, repeating over and over: *'It is only for good. It is meant only for good. Only good can come.'* As I did my work day after day I clung to these words as a drowning man to a straw. It was all I could hold to, the only thing I could grasp in the midst of an overwhelming tide of affairs.

"If I repeated the words a dozen times, I repeated them a thousand times. The more I did so, the more I could feel a growing conviction within me that they were true, that the goodness the experience held was going to be greater than my greatest expectation. This goodness did not appear all at once. It became apparent only degree by degree. I found a foundation of strength and faith, courage and conviction in developing anew within my heart and mind. I found an assurance I had never before known concerning God's love for me and His goodness. I found that I was unconsciously radiating to others more of this conviction and assurance in God's goodness. Persons noticed the change and expressed amazement concerning it.

"As the months went by, I knew that a deep transformation within me was taking place. I knew that there was a newness of consciousness, a quickened perception of God. The specific outcome of the situation became less important while the good inherent within it became all-important and increasingly apparent.

"Now, although there are a few details to be worked out, fringes of the problem to be smoothed out, I am at peace and exceedingly happy because I know that only increasing good has come and will continue to come as time goes by. *'Only good can come'* is my thorough conviction and faith. The meaning of the words has been so deeply and completely impressed upon me that it remains with me now as a constant conviction, a living faith."

This was so evident in the face, manner, bearing, and the voice of the Truth student that my heart leaped for joy. I knew something of the situation confronting the young woman and I knew that she had had to release a loved one with whom she had shared many joyous years. She had watched this loved one leave her life, watched another woman take her place. I knew that through continued prayer and steadfast faith she had realized release for herself from a bondage that came to light only through the outer upheaval occasioned. Through prayer she had truly overcome all human feeling of envy and jealousy and loss.

Her parting words to me that day were spoken from her heart, and the truth of them shone through her beautiful, expressive eyes: "I have only love within me for these persons. I wish them only the very best of everything—peace, happiness, success, all the desires of their hearts. For myself, I have a freedom now that I have not felt in many months. I am in love with life now as never before. I have never before known how wonderfully good the goodness of God is!"

This almost miraculous attitude was the result of faithful and steadfast prayer and the diligent application of Truth principles. It had meant days and nights of constancy of spirit and trust in God's goodness, repetitions by the hundreds, yes—thousands, that *"Only good can come,"* and a continued acting out of Truth in daily living.

What this Truth student accomplished, anyone can accomplish—you can accomplish. Regardless of the type of experience that you find facing you, whether it concerns personal relationships, finances, or well-being, you can be a similar overcomer, a similar staunch and unwavering conqueror through the Christ Spirit dwelling in you.

You can begin right now to come into the realization of your heart's desire for freedom, joy, peace, supply, for any good of any kind, by simply affirming in faith, *"Only good is in this situation. Only good can come."* Repeat it over and over. Then become still, open, and receptive to God's love and wisdom and guidance. *"Only good can come."* Let the words be impressed so indelibly upon your consciousness that nothing else can find room to enter or lodge therein. *"Only good can come."*

It makes no difference what the appearance. It matters not what the seeming. It simply remains with you to hold fast to God in the face of all that is before you, in the midst of any and all outer conflict, confusion, or trial. Only good can come! Only good can come; for God, the good, is all there is!

Recall the experiences of Joseph, son of Jacob, and of his being sold as a slave, thrown into prison, and forgotten by all those who were of his own household. Throughout every unjust, trying situation we see that he must have held to the faith that only good would come, that regardless of the malevolence, regardless of the difficulties involved, only good would come.

We know that good did come to Joseph. We know that he arose to the high position of ruler over all the land of Egypt, next to Pharaoh in authority and in honor, and that through his faith every experience was turned to good not only for himself but for all the people of the kingdom. We remember his meaningful words to his brothers, "And as for you, ye meant evil against me; but God meant it for good."

Think for a moment of another who knew within his heart that only good could come. Jesus of Nazareth in the midst of innumerable trials and suffering held fast to the faith that only good could come.

Perhaps His words to the Father were a bit different than these we are using right now. Instead of "Only good can come," He said something more in the vein of "Thy will be done,

Father, for it is good, and good only for me and
for all." The meaning is the same. His faith was
the same. His trust was the same. The principle
was the same. He knew that in spite of the appearances only good could come, that this is all
God intends.

I have found that when I am uncertain about
the outcome of some effort, the words "Thank
You, God" help lift my heart, and an unexpected blessing always follows. If I am anxious
about the attitude or behavior of a loved one
or a friend, the words "Thank You, God" remind me that He is ever active, ever present,
and all powerful within all His children, and
my concern is wholly unjustified.

When I am in doubt about meeting a bus
on time I find the words "Thank You, God"
give me the assurance and calm I need, and
ample time suddenly becomes available. When
I am in doubt about the success of a new recipe,
the words "Thank You, God" make the cook-
ing efforts easier, and the results are unfailingly
better than I anticipated. Before I take the
morning mail from the box, "Thank You, God"
prepares the way for me to give as well as receive a blessing. Before I answer the ringing

telephone, "Thank You, God" again opens the way for me to give and receive some great good.

By this I do not mean that every bit of news I receive is encouraging, that every message is positive and uplifting, that every day's activities are perfect, devoid of difficulty, but my habit of saying "Thank You, God" establishes me in an attitude of thanksgiving that never fails to turn all things toward good, and bring me a reward of increased faith and understanding.

However strange it may seem to you to say "Thank You, God" while confronted by the appearance of sickness, weakness, discouragement, and lack, try it! In boldness and in faith declare silently and aloud, *"Thank You, God, for well-being"* (or, for strength, or supply, or wisdom). Declare it during the monotony of routine, and the day will suddenly be blessed with new interest. Say it during times of small temptations and in the face of strong negation. Live and move and have your being in an attitude of thanksgiving. It will bring rewards you cannot begin to envision!

Take heart and stand firm with One who is ever encouraging you to follow Him and walk in His ways. Say with Him now in His name,

"Only good can come." Speak it quietly but faithfully and with authority, *"Only good can come."*

Only good is intended for you. Only good is God's intent and purpose in your life and affairs. The way you can begin to accept this good is through sincere use of your indwelling faith, through steadfast affirmation of the words, *"Only good can come."* Repeat them aloud, right now.

As you do this you will find that Truth becomes potent and real and tangible, a sure foundation in your mind and heart, a strong basis for every other word, for every act. Truth will renew you in body. It will adjust every situation, heal every condition, right every circumstance, transform your life. It will prove to you that the goodness of God is unlimited, infinite, unchangeable, and enduring.

"Only good can come," only good can come to you. You are God's own cherished and beloved, for whom good—and good only—has been prepared. Claim it now with all the faith in your heart. *"Only good can come!"* "Praise ye Jehovah . . . for he is good . . . his lovingkindness *endureth* for ever."

Meditation for Self-Help

If you are confronted by a situation that seems impossible of solution, if you seem to be up against a stone wall, be assured that there is a way out of the difficulty.

No matter what anyone has said, no matter how you have felt in the past, no matter what the circumstances and how complex they appear, there is a solution, there is a way.

Summon into your mind and heart all the faith you can at this moment, and speak the words, *"There is a way."* Repeat the words in quietness and confidence. Repeat them silently and aloud, *"There is a way, there is a way."*

There is a way to inner peace and stability. There is a way to control your feelings and emotions. There is a way to rise above false desires or habits. There is a way to re-establish your prosperity. There is a way to realize your wholeness and vitality. There is a way to enjoy love and right companionship. There is a way to right attainment of every good desire of your heart. "I will . . . make a way."

"I will even make a way in the wilderness." This is the Father's promise to you now; and as you listen in prayer, in quietness, and in faith, you shall not only hear this reassurance but also see the way to follow God's guidance. You will be provided with all the strength, courage, and wisdom you need to go forward to peace, victory, and accomplishment.

There is a way. As you turn to the Father in faith, knowing this truth, affirming it with deep sincerity and quiet confidence, it shall be made plain to you. Jesus said, "I am the way, and the truth, and the life."

Be still and listen. Be still and have faith and confidence in your indwelling Lord, who is your perfect guide. Be still and open your mind and heart to the One who longs to lead you and bless you. "And thine ears shall hear a word behind thee, saying, This is the way, walk ye in it; when ye turn to the right hand, and when ye turn to the left."

There is a way. There is a way for you. It is now clear, visible to you. It lies ahead of you, it leads upward.

"Fear thou not, for I am with thee; be not dismayed, for I am thy God; I will strengthen thee; yea, I will help thee." "I will . . . make a way."

Accept Your Good

NOT LONG AGO a man remarked to a Truth teacher, "A few years ago the doctors told me that I would never again be able to hear, even with the best of hearing aids, and that I must learn to lip-read. Through the study of Unity teachings and now in this classwork I find myself able to hear every word you speak and I am hearing better, more clearly, all the time."

This is just one example of what is constantly taking place in many Truth classes, an example seen by many Truth teachers and students throughout the world. It is one specific example of a Truth student's hearing the Truth of Being, believing in it, and then providing the constant, steadfast receiving consciousness that accepts Truth as a tangible, living, and manifest reality.

All that we desire, all that we can ever envision or hope to attain is already provided for us; it is already available and will ever be awaiting our acceptance. This is true whether it concerns the body, home, or business; whether conditions and situations seem desperate and difficult; whether circumstances seem to be hopelessly entangled and confused; or whether the attainment of the desires and visions of our hearts seem impossible, beyond hope of realization.

The only condition on which this manifest good is dependent for complete outer expression is the condition of consciousness. As explained by one Truth teacher and writer, "The Spirit can do for us only what it can do through us. Unless we are able to provide the consciousness, Spirit cannot make the gift." If the consciousness is filled with impressions of negative appearances, it is not the kind of consciousness that can receive the good gifts that the Giver desires to offer to His beloved sons. If the consciousness is full of doubt and permeated by anxiety and fear, it is not the kind of consciousness that provides a free channel for the overflowing Christ heritage of goodness.

There is something we can do, however, to provide the right kind of consciousness, the receiving consciousness. This something we can do is not in any way a personal manipulation of thought by so many words and phrases that are uttered repetitiously and mechanically. It is, rather, a "letting go and letting God;" that is, a letting go of all preconceived thoughts and conjectures in favor of letting God reform, reshape, and remold our consciousness according to His divine plan.

This process begins when we consciously close the door on our old misconceptions and allow admittance only to beautiful ideas and words of Truth, life, love, and peace. It then continues with our willingness to become consciously impressionable, pliable, and receptive to the divine inner power that is above and beyond our human understanding.

The Spirit itself will form this receiving consciousness within us, as we give it free access to our minds and hearts. The Spirit is more than eager and more than abundantly ready to remold, transform, and renew our consciousness if we will simply let it do so without any human forcing of the will!

Help yourself to become receptive right now by giving yourself wholeheartedly to the presence of Spirit, our Father-Mother God. Speak quietly to yourself, saying, *"I now give my whole being—spirit, mind, body, and affairs —to You, Father. I now let go and let You form in me the perfect receiving consciousness. Of myself I can do nothing; therefore, I willingly let You do the transforming that is needful and desirable. Mold my consciousness anew. I would be meek, lowly, humble, and pliable to Your inner working of good. I would be utterly flexible, in harmony with Your movement of love within me. Fashion me anew in mind and heart. I would be impressionable and malleable to Your desires. Express through me according to Your highest plan for me. I let You form the perfect receiving consciousness within me now."*

When you have spoken these words quietly and gently with your whole heart centered upon them, be still, let go, and let God. Strive no longer to imagine what the results may be. Loose all, leave all, and let God move within your consciousness. He will remold, refashion, and re-create in you the perfect receiving consciousness for life, peace, love, joy, beauty, wisdom, and abundance of good.

Jesus is the perfect example of the perfect receiving consciousness. His manner, His attitude, His words, and His teachings never bespoke strain, strife, personal power, or human willfulness. His life is an expression of a perfect continual receiving from God. He was the perfect channel, the perfect vessel, the perfect embodiment through which God could move and have His being.

Most of us want to be good givers. We are eager to share all the fine and lovely things of life with others, but we sometimes forget that we must take the time and thought for receiving. Being a good receiver is not a complicated task, but a matter of simple application. As one Truth student puts it: "Take time, every day, quietly to let God give to you. Be still, sit quiet, and simply say to the loving Father, '*I am ready to receive, dear Father. I am ready to receive all the good You wish to give to me. I am receiving, now.*'"

Learn to be a good receiver. Become open and receptive to your good through prayer, through affirming, "*I am receiving. I am receiving now.*" As you do so, you open the gates of your mind and heart, you open the long-closed passages of the soul, you enlarge and expand the cramped quarters of your being until they are amply ready to receive the bounty of God's goodness, prepared, and ready for overflowing.

Do not let yourself become concerned about whether you have previously spoken, acted, lived in a manner worthy of receiving God's good. Do not be anxious if you feel you may have taken many wrong steps or perhaps misunderstood God's guidance or misinterpreted His leadings, for nothing, absolutely nothing in the outer world, can prevent your acceptance of God's good which is ever at hand, awaiting your claim.

No place that we may go or be is beyond the reach of the ever-present One and His goodness. No complication of outer circumstances can prevent this all-present good from reaching you, from lifting and sustaining and helping you. No human mistake can separate you from the constantly present goodness of God, once you acknowledge its presence and accept its reality.

Acknowledge and accept the presence and power and goodness of God right now, without further delay, and they will become manifest in your life. Right where you are, right within the circumstances surrounding you, right within the appearance of failure, right in the middle of the darkest human experience is the

goodness of God that is His will for you, His
own beloved child.

Do not become discouraged if the results of
your affirmations and prayers do not appear to
take the shape and form you think is right and
advantageous. Remember, after Jesus arose
from His prayer in the Garden of Gethsemane
it was needful that He continue in His acceptance of the goodness of the will of God
throughout His trial before the Sanhedrin,
throughout much scourging and the ridicule of
the angry mobs, throughout perhaps a human
temptation to give in to the suggestions of
Pontius Pilate, throughout the sorrow and pain
of the Crucifixion itself.

Yet His heart must have turned and returned throughout all the outer confusion to a
quiet inner acceptance of the goodness of God
and His promises, to the truth that this goodness was inviolable and absolutely sure of manifestation. He must have known that His part in
bringing it forth was a faithful and constant
acceptance of it as true and inviolable and absolutely sure and certain, irrespective of every
outer evidence to the contrary.

There is nothing that God cannot make

right, nothing He cannot heal, restore, renew, supply, or provide if we will but become open, receptive, and obedient to His workings. As we become quiet and still, as we persistently and faithfully relax and let go and let God, we present ourselves in an acceptable way to the Holy Spirit's anointing of our consciousness. We let the oils of joy and love and gladness soften all the hardened issues of our life. We become wholly receptive to the Truths of Being. The results then speak—indeed, shout— for themselves and proclaim to all, "This is my beloved Son, in whom I am well pleased."

It is the Father's good pleasure to give His children the fullness of the kingdom. Nothing so delights God as the willingness of His children to receive. Nothing pleases the Giver more than to find an open and receptive channel through which to pour His blessings for manifestation. It is the Father's great ecstasy and joy to find freedom of activity within and throughout His creations. It is our part to cultivate and present the constant receiving consciousness in order that we may delight our Father. He Himself is that measure of All-Good that eagerly awaits our acceptance!

Determine this day, dear friend, to accept the goodness of God as never before, to accept it in the Spirit of Jesus Christ, in His manner of conviction, in His attitude of steadfastness and faith. Say, in a continuing consciousness of acceptance of good, *"Father, Thy will be done. Thy good and wonderful and perfect will be done."* As you do so, you will realize more clearly than ever the goodness and beauty and perfection of God's will, its unlimitedness, its all-inclusive upliftment and blessing of your heart, your mind, your body temple, your life and affairs.

God is good and good only! Let your heart and mind sing the words. Say them silently, say them aloud, say them all through the day and night and until you realize the fullness of truth they contain. God loves you infinitely, dear friend, far beyond your highest conception of this truth. God is good and good only, now and forevermore, and ever at hand with and within you, to help you into continually greater acceptance of the blessings prepared for you.

In the light of this truth, in your awareness of the goodness and perfection of the will of

God, no appearance or evidence of negation will stand. Its former conclusiveness and finality will suddenly be dissolved and exist no more. All you will see is the goodness of God, the love of God, the peace of God, the joy of God. All you will feel will be His goodness, His loving kindness, the peace and joy and happiness that He gives. There will be naught else than Him. There will simply be God and God only, good and good only in expression and manifestation in and through you, His beloved son and heir. Your will and His will will be one—good, and good only!

Meditation for Self-Help

Plenty is my heritage. Faith, love, joy, peace, good in every form are mine from God. There is no lack in the kingdom of God. I praise and bless God's bounty. I rejoice that plenty is my heritage.

God, my all-loving Father, enriches my mind with plenty of divine ideas—ideas of wisdom, light, and inspiration.

God blesses my body with plenty of life, strength, wholeness, energy.

God blesses my affairs with plenty in every conceivable form, including food, clothing, and housing.

I have plenty, plenty, plenty, for God is my supply.

Plenty of every good and needful substance is all about me. It enriches my mind; it sustains my body; it overflows into my home; it prospers my activities; it fills my purse; it enlarges my bank account. Plenty is my heritage. It is my heritage as a child of the Father. I claim and accept it now.

I do not strive or struggle; I entertain no doubts; I ask no questions. I let go and let my good come to me as God directs.

I do not seek anything unjustly. I do not beg
or plead or scheme. I acknowledge the truth that
God is the Spirit of plenty, the giver of all good,
and I open my heart to receive of His every-
where present, abundant, and all-sufficient
supply.

I cannot lack anything. It is a divine impos-
sibility. There is no such thing as insufficiency
in Spirit. God cannot be inadequate, insufficient.
Therefore, I, His child and heir, cannot know
inadequacy or insufficiency.

Plenty is my heritage. I willingly co-operate
with the law of plenty by seeking for new ways
to give. I give of myself, my time, my ability,
my talents. I give honestly, sincerely, naturally.
I give generously, lovingly, in the manner and to
the degree that I can. As I give, I see my fund
and reserve of plenty grow and become greater.

I remember that "just enough" is not my
heritage. Plenty is my free gift from my loving
Father. I do not accept less. I open wide my consciousness to the truth that God loves me and
gives to me in overflowing measure. I am willing and expectant.

Plenty is my heritage, for my supply is from

God. Good is flowing into my life from every direction. The very windows of heaven are opened to me.

Plenty is my heritage!

p. 87 - Send to Mike